Body Beautiful

Body Beautiful

Recovering the Biblical View of the Church

Melvin Tinker and
Nathan Buttery

Authentic
LIFESTYLE

Copyright © Melvin Tinker and Nathan Buttery 2003

First published in 2003 by Authentic Lifestyle

09 08 07 06 05 04 03   7 6 5 4 3 2 1

Authentic Lifestyle is an imprint of Authentic Media,
PO Box 300, Carlisle, Cumbria CA3 0QS, UK
Box 1047, Waynesboro, GA 30830-2047, USA
www.paternoster-publishing.com

The right of Melvin Tinker and Nathan Buttery to be
identified as the Authors of this Work has been
asserted by them in accordance with
Copyright, Designs and Patents Act 1988

British Library Cataloguing in Publication Data

A catalogue record for this book is available from the British
Library

ISBN 1-85078-465-5

Cover design by Sam Redwood
Printed in Great Britain by
Cox and Wyman Ltd., Reading

Dedication

*To the members and staff of St John's, Newland,
Riverside and St Faith's with whom it is a privilege
to be fellow workers in the Gospel.*

Contents

Foreword

I have many books on my shelves about evangelism, but I am not impressed by any of them if the authors are not practitioners. Likewise, I have many books on the church, but many of them fail to carry conviction because they have not been written by church leaders. It is one thing to write airily about the church, but quite another to lead a large and growing church humbly and effectively in the heart of the inner city. But that is what Melvin Tinker, the Vicar of St John's, Newlands, Hull, and his colleague Nathan Buttery have done. And I am impressed by the book not least because I have helped to lead an evangelistic outreach in that church and have experienced its vitality. These men know what they are talking about.

They set out in what looks to me like a series of sermons, to write eleven chapters on the church, Christ's church, which the powers of Hades will never be able to quell. They rarely refer to any other books on the subject but confine themselves to three things. They expound a variety of passages of the New Testament which speak about the church. They apply the material sensitively to the readers, as they would have done to those who heard the sermons. And they often give attractive and sometimes memorable instructions which illuminate the topic. They are concerned to allow the Bible to speak for itself, and while they do not tell us all it has to say about

the church, and are clearly not enamoured of its Catholic
or Charismatic manifestations, they succeed in giving
thoughtful and often gripping expositions of the passage they are considering. You do not often find that in
a book. I am delighted to see it. They allow Scripture to
make its own impact on the reader, and incidentally give
brilliant examples of how to expound it, which many a
clergyman could profit from. I hope the book will clear
away a lot of misconceptions, thrill people again with
the bride of Christ that the church is meant to be, and
maybe encourage them to go to St John's, Newland to
see for themselves that the church there genuinely man-
ifests many of the marks of the church about which they
write. This is a book to buy, to ponder, and to embody in
the life of your church.

Michael Green
Wycliffe Hall
Oxford University

Preface

Several years ago when Pepsi Cola was launched in China with an all-out marketing campaign, the marketing managers were at a complete loss as to why their famous slogan 'Come Alive with Pepsi' wasn't having an impact. Sales were hardly moving at all. Then they discovered why. The slogan was in fact having a tremendous impact, but a negative one. For what had happened was that the translator had rendered 'Come Alive with Pepsi' as 'Pepsi brings your relatives back from the dead.'

Cross-cultural communication is a tremendous challenge, but so is intercultural communication. The associations a word or concept has in the minds of one group might have an entirely different range of associations in the minds of another group *within the same culture*. This most certainly applies to the notion of 'church'. We would suspect that a book with the word 'church' in the title, unless accompanied by dynamic adjectives like 'The Purpose Driven Church' or 'The Outreaching Church' is not going to draw a large readership. This is partly because the word 'church' has become associated with inertia, committees, reports, top heavy organisational structures and the like. Even when thought of primarily in theological terms, the associations are not all that attractive either, conjuring up images of denominational squabbles, high-ranking dignitaries, and ecumenical speak, all of which seem a million light years away from the concerns of rank and file Christians trying to live out their lives in the light of the Gospel.

What this book seeks to do is to recapture in a popular and readily accessible manner the vibrant vision that the Bible offers of what the church is and can be. As we take a fresh look at the teaching of Jesus and his apostles, we will be struck by how wide of the mark are many of the contemporary evangelical views of the church. It is easy for any of us to allow ideas to develop, which over time become part of the received tradition, without going back to the Bible to check things out. This book is an attempt to do just that.

While providing a secure biblical and theological basis for our exploration, we shall be working through some of the practical implications this has for churches as they find themselves in an increasingly postmodern secularised society. To assist in this, Bible studies have been included in the latter part of the book for individual or group use based on the different passages expounded in the first half of the book. We would encourage people to be 'Berean-like' in their approach and check out for themselves what we are saying. Hopefully you too will be as surprised, challenged and refreshed as we have been.

We would like to express our appreciation to all those who have helped us in this venture: first rate colleagues on the pastoral-teaching team of St John's with whom it is a joy to work; the congregations in which we serve, whose members try and model many of the qualities we shall be discussing in these pages; our wives, Heather and Debbie, who are our best critics. Thanks too go to Shirley Godbold, our administrator, for checking the manuscript, who also ensures that many of the practical day-to-day tasks in the life of the church get done. Most of all we are grateful to God who in his mercy has called us to be members of the Body Beautiful – the Church.

Melvin Tinker and Nathan Buttery
St John's Newland
Hull
Soli Deo Gloria

1

What is the Church?
Matthew 16:13–20

When Jesus came to the region of Caesarea Philippi, he asked his disciples, 'Who do people say the Son of Man is?'

They replied, 'Some say John the Baptist; others say Elijah; and still others, Jeremiah or one of the prophets.'

'But what about you?' he asked. 'Who do you say I am?'

Simon Peter answered, 'You are the Christ, the Son of the living God.'

Jesus replied, 'Blessed are you, Simon son of Jonah, for this was not revealed to you by man, but by my Father in hea-ven. And I tell you that you are Peter, and on this rock I will build my church, and the gates of Hades will not over-come it. I will give you the keys of the kingdom of heaven; whatever you bind on earth will be bound in heaven, and whatever you loose on earth will be loosed in heaven.' Then he warned his disciples not to tell anyone that he was the Christ.

A Culture of Non-Commitment

Here is an extract from an article that appeared in a British national newspaper several years ago:

> In an average English village today, Anglican worship has become little more than a dying bourgeois cult. A small cluster of motor cars may be seen outside the parish church when the service is in progress; the bells still ring joyously across the fields and meadows on Sunday mornings and Sunday evenings, but fewer and fewer heed them, and those who do are predominantly middle-class, female and elderly. It must be desperately disheartening, and the Vicar often gives the impression of being dispirited and forlorn. Whatever zeal he may have had as an ordinand soon gets dissipated in an atmosphere of domestic care and indifference on the part of his flock. Small wonder, then, that in the pulpit he has little to say except to repeat the same old clerical banalities. He doubtless feels himself to be redundant. The villagers stoically die without his ministrations; they would resent any interruption to their evening telly if he ventured to make a call . . . In large cities the situation is not dissimilar.

So wrote Malcolm Muggeridge some twenty to thirty years ago. The situation now, of course, is even worse, with the major denominations losing something like 1,500 members a week and with only 2 per cent of the population present in an Anglican church on any given Sunday in the UK and 8 per cent overall. The poor image that the church has in the minds of many is often a sad reflection of the reality.

In some ways the church is not alone in its struggle to attract and keep members. We live in a society of 'reluctant joiners', steadily producing a culture of non-commitment.

Consequently couples are increasingly choosing to opt out of their marriage commitment, with the result that in Britain cohabiting has more than doubled in the last twenty-five years and almost one in two marriages now ends in divorce. Charities are finding it very difficult to get people to work for them on a voluntary basis. All political parties and trade unions have seen a sharp fall in membership. The days of missionaries working overseas for life now seem numbered as they are increasingly replaced with short-term placements. This is the problem of non-commitment.

To a certain extent much of this is understandable. After all, the degree to which we are willing to commit ourselves to something is dependent upon how highly we value it, which in turn depends upon how we view it. It certainly would seem that one of the reasons why even Bible-believing Christians often seem reluctant to give their all to the church is because they have never understood what being church really means. That is one of the main purposes of this book: to enable us to discover afresh, and maybe for some of us for the very first time, what a glorious, breathtaking and exciting thing the church is. So we begin by going back to consider what Jesus himself had to say on the subject in Matthew 16.

Popes or People?

This is a passage over which much ink, if not blood, has been spilt, mainly over questions such as whether Jesus is here instigating the papacy with Peter as the first pope. To be frank, that is to miss entirely the main point that Jesus is making. The focus is not on the relationship between Jesus and Peter as his Vicar on earth, but between Jesus and his people of which Peter is a representative. In other words, the church. In particular we shall be concentrating on what is in many ways the key verse, verse 18, where Jesus says: 'And I tell you that you are Peter, and on this rock I will build my church, and the gates of Hades will not overcome it.'

Which Church?

Let's begin by asking: just what is this 'church' which Jesus speaks of as '*my* church'? To answer that question we must understand that in both the Greek and Hebrew it is a word which simply means a 'crowd', or a 'gathering' – an assembly of people (*ekklesia/qahal*). In Acts 19, for example, Luke in verse 32 describes the mob that was rioting in Ephesus as 'the church'. They weren't Christians, so this is not particularly a religious word; here it is used to describe a crowd on the rampage. Later on, in verse 39, a court of officials is called 'the church'. If Luke were around today and describing the cabinet meeting of a city council he would no doubt talk about the 'church' meeting in the town hall! Therefore, at this stage we can say that 'church' is nothing more or less than a gathering of people. If there is no gathering, then by definition there is no church.

But of course here Jesus is not talking about any old gathering. He speaks of 'my gathering'. As we look at the rest of the passage we find the answers to two very important questions: First, *how* does Jesus gather his people? And second, *where* does Jesus gather his people, his church?

The 'How?' Question

The answer to the question: 'How are God's people gathered?' is that they are gathered by Christ himself.

Jesus emphatically says, '*I* will build my church.' This building up of a people occurs in two ways: quantitatively, in terms of numbers being added to the 'Jesus crowd', and qualitatively, as these people increasingly begin to reflect the character of Jesus himself – after all they are *his* people. The means that Jesus uses to achieve both of these ends is the same: it is by the proclamation of the Gospel; that is how he calls people to belong to his crowd. In fact the very word 'church', (*ekklesia*) suggests this, for it means those who are *called* together.

This whole discussion between Jesus and his disciples underscores the fact that he calls people to himself, and so to each other, by a *revelatory* message. Here they are in Caesarea Philippi, non-Jew country, which may in itself be significant, pointing to the fact that Jesus also intends to have Gentiles amongst his people and not just Jews. It is then when suddenly Jesus asks his followers, 'Who do people say that I am?' After they have reeled off various contemporary theories about his identity, that he is some sort of spectacular prophet for example, Jesus asks them directly, 'Yes, but who do *you* say that I am?' In other words, what do you my followers believe about me? As usual Peter is the self-appointed spokesman for them all, as we see in verse 16: 'You are the Christ, the Son of the living God.' What is Jesus reply? 'Well done, Peter, what a clever chap you are, how perceptive of you'? Not a bit of it. 'You are really blessed Simon son of Jonah for this was not revealed to you by man, but by my Father in heaven.' It's as if to say, 'It is not because you are the son of *your* father that you have insight so as to have made such a profound confession of faith, but it is *my* Father who has revealed this to you.' It is then we come to a little play on words, a pun: 'I am going to reveal something to you, from now on you are *Petros* and on this *petra* I am going to build my church.' Your name is Rock and on this 'rock' I am going to gather my people.

What is That All About?

Consider for a moment what it is that Simon Peter has just confessed. It is in essence the Gospel, the Good News about who Jesus is – 'The Son of the living God' – and what he came to do – to be 'the Christ', the one whom God has anointed to carry out his special mission of saving people from their sins. It is through that message, and indeed this person, Peter, that Jesus began and continues to gather people to himself.

Think of the day of Pentecost. It was Peter who stood up, proclaimed the Gospel and three thousand people were added to the church that day in Jerusalem. Here we see with total clarity that it is as the word of the Gospel is proclaimed and believed in the power of the Holy Spirit, that the church is built. What is more, it is the same Gospel in all its richness that continues to build God's people in terms of their spiritual life. That is why this same Peter, the 'Rock', writes in his first letter to several Christian gatherings, 'You have been born again, not of perishable seed, but of the imperishable, through the living and enduring word of God . . . this is the word that was preached to you' (1 Pet. 1:23), speaking of how these people were gathered in the first place, and then that they are to grow by 'craving pure spiritual milk' (2:1). People are saved by the Gospel and sanctified by the Gospel.

Now we can see why all true Christian ministry is to be Word-centred ministry, teaching, sharing and proclaiming the truth about Jesus. Today in the west people are wondering why there is church decline, in stark contrast say, to Africa or Asia where thousands are being drawn to Christ on a daily basis. There are plenty of reasons to be sure, but one thing is for certain: many churches here have simply lost confidence in the Gospel message and the belief that through the power of that message Christ builds his church. While it is true that we have to work hard at our communication skills and reduce to a minimum the gap between ourselves and the non-Christian, nonetheless if the claims of Jesus Christ are not presented clearly and with conviction, or are obscured by other things, then we should not be surprised if we do not see churches grow as Jesus intends them to grow. Obviously one can grow a so-called 'church' on all sorts of foundations – turn it into a social club, or revolve it around some entertaining personality – but it will not be a church built upon the rock Jesus speaks of as we see it embodied in the person and confession of Peter, the rock of the Gospel. That is what our African brothers and sisters know and experience. That is also why they pray so much, asking *Christ* to build his church. They have not been busy dismantling the Bible like many in the west, or being half-hearted in prayer, so only a handful turn up to the prayer meeting; they still believe it and they proclaim it and so it spreads like wildfire. Surely that is the conviction that we need to recapture. Christians are gathered together by the Gospel.

The 'Where?' Question

We now come to our second question: 'Where is the church gathered?' The answer: around Jesus. Christ gathers his people around himself. Therefore, where Jesus is, that is where his 'crowd' or 'church' is.

So let us ask: where is Jesus now? Because that is where we will find his true church. There are in fact two parts to the answer.

First of all Jesus is in heaven, seated at the right hand of God, surrounded by his people, all those who have died trusting in him. This includes believers from the Old Testament period right up to the present day. The writer to the Hebrews, in chapter 12, speaks of this as the heavenly Zion, 'the church of the firstborn enrolled in heaven'. That is the primary church which Jesus is building and which the gates of Hades, that is death, cannot destroy. How can it? After all, these people have already cheated death since they are now alive with Christ in heaven never to die again.

As the Gospel is proclaimed, and people believe it, then they are automatically signed up to the everlasting church of heaven. Do you realise that if you are a Christian believer, your name is already on the heavenly membership list even as you read this and nothing can take your name off it? Do you not find that warmly reassuring? No matter what might happen to us on earth as individuals and no matter what might happen to the local church to which we belong (whether it grows or closes) the Christian's place amongst God's people in heaven is guaranteed.

Indeed, it is to this church that the Nicene creed refers: 'We believe in one holy, catholic, apostolic, church.' For clarity's sake it should be said that this has nothing to do with Roman Catholicism. 'Catholic' simply means 'universal': a group made up of all sorts of different people. That, of course, is exactly what the church meeting in heaven is made up of – people from every race and from every age (Rev. 7:9). Furthermore it is *one*. There are not several churches meeting in heaven, only a single crowd meeting around the one throne. That is why we say we *believe* in this church, because we cannot yet see it. One day we shall and what a day that will be! We have not yet seen a church that even begins to match up to that one, pure, vibrant church, pulsating with love and unadorned beauty, engrossed in selfless adoration and praise of the one who died for them. This church can never be described as boring. Do not say church is dead and boring. It is the only place in the universe where there is true life and excitement.

But secondly, while Jesus is present bodily in heaven with his children gathered around him, he is also present on earth by his Spirit. This means that when his people are gathered together by his Word, Jesus is actually moving amongst them just as surely and just as real as when he was present with his disciples there in Caeserea Philippi. We can't see him, but he is present nonetheless. Jesus says something to this effect in Matthew 18, the only other place where Jesus uses the term 'church': 'Where two or three are gathered in my name [there is the Gospel again], there I am in their midst.' Not, 'I may be there on the odd occasion', I *am* in their midst. That is truly an awesome thought. Here is a description of the Jesus who is with you as you gather together with other Christians each Sunday as church: 'When I turned I saw seven golden lampstands, and among the lampstands was someone "like a son of man", dressed in a robe reaching down to his feet and with a golden sash round his chest. His head and hair were white like wool, as white as snow, and his eyes were like blazing fire' (Rev. 1:12–14). The lampstands, we are told in verse 20, are local churches, and Jesus is moving amongst each one of them! Knowing that, how does that affect our feeling about being with other believers? If we want to meet with Jesus in his risen power, then we must meet with his people, for that is where we shall find him.

While, therefore, there is only *one* church in heaven (which Jesus is building and the gates of death cannot harm), there are *many* churches on earth, which should be reflecting – mirroring – the church in heaven. We might want to think of the relationship between each local church and the one, true, heavenly church like a spider plant. There is the 'mother plant', which sends out a number of runners, and at the end of each of its runners is a small plantlet. The heavenly church is like that mother plant, with each Gospel-believing congregation being an offshoot and a replica (albeit an imperfect one) of the church now meeting around the throne of Christ in glory.

Working It Out

What are some of the implications of this lofty view of the church?

First of all, we must get our thinking right.

It means that by definition a denomination cannot be a church, because it is not a gathering. Strictly speaking there is no 'Church of England', there is a federation of churches called the Church of England. The Reformers understood and enshrined it in article 19 of the Anglican 'Thirty-Nine Articles' of belief: 'The visible church of Christ [as contrast to the invisible heavenly church] is a congregation of faithful men [that is Christian believers], in which the pure word of God is preached and the sacraments duly administered.' Which is really all that we have been arguing. The church of which you are a member is not *part* of the church in England, it is *a* church in England, a colony or outcrop of Christ's church in heaven.

Secondly, we must get our priorities right.

Our passionate concern should be to be working with Christ to build his church in heaven. Certainly he is the one who does the building, but he does it through people. Evangelism must therefore be central to all that the church does – reaching out to others, prayerfully and lovingly, so that they might be enrolled in the great gathering of heaven. Nothing less than their eternal well-being depends on it. Churches are not meant to be forever looking inward, only concerned with maintenance, but always looking outward, being engaged in mission. That is what this matter of the keys in verse 19 is all about: 'I will give you the keys of the kingdom of heaven, whatever you bind on earth has been bound in heaven and what is loosed on earth has been loosed in heaven.' In Luke 11, Jesus castigates the religious rulers of his day for taking away the key of knowledge so as to prevent people from entering God's kingdom (Lk. 11:52). But Peter – and now all Christians through proclaiming the Gospel – has the key to true knowledge so that those who believe it are set free and those who continue to reject it are bound.

However, as well as having an outward focus on the world in proclaiming the Gospel, we should also have an inward concern for each other in living the Gospel. We should treasure the local gathering of Christ's people as he treasures it. The Lord Jesus loves his people meeting with him, and if he thought it worthwhile to give his life to enable that to happen then the least we can do is to have the courtesy to meet and serve each other in whatever ways we can.

'I *will* build my church,' says Jesus, 'and the gates of Hades *will* not prevail against it.'

Can we hear more encouraging words about the church than those?

2

God and the Church
1 Peter 2:4–12

As you come to him, the living Stone – rejected by men but chosen by God and precious to him – you also, like living stones, are being built into a spiritual house to be a holy priesthood, offering spiritual sacrifices acceptable to God through Jesus Christ. For in Scripture it says:

> *'See, I lay a stone in Zion,*
> *a chosen and precious cornerstone,*
> *and the one who trusts in him*
> *will never be put to shame.'*

Now to you who believe, this stone is precious. But to those who do not believe,

> *'The stone the builders rejected*
> *has become the capstone'*

and,

> *'A stone that causes men to stumble*
> *and a rock that makes them fall.'*

*They stumble because they disobey the message – which is also
what they were destined for.*

*But you are a chosen people, a royal priesthood, a holy
nation, a people belonging to God, that you may declare the
praises of him who called you out of darkness into his wonderful light. Once you were not a people, but now you are the people of God; once you had not received mercy, but now you have
received mercy.*

*Dear friends, I urge you, as aliens and strangers in the
world, to abstain from sinful desires, which war against your
soul. Live such good lives among the pagans that, though they
accuse you of doing wrong, they may see your good deeds and
glorify God on the day he visits us.*

Her name was Blandina. She was a Gallic slave living at
the end of the second century. She was also a recent con-
vert to Christianity. Because of this she was forced to
watch the murder of her Christian companions, then
heated on a gridiron, thrown to the wild beasts in the
arena and finally impaled on a stake. She actually died
praying for her persecutors.

It was pretty much the same story repeated over and
over again since this new faith had burst upon the
Roman Empire around AD 33. Persecution of one kind or
another. What sort of thoughts might come flooding into
the minds of Christians living under those conditions, as
indeed, many are living today? Would they not be
thoughts like these: 'Could we have got it all wrong? Are
we so special to God? and 'Where is he?' If you are a pastor ministering to such believers, what are you going to
say to them, 'Oh, don't worry. It won't last for ever. Hang
in there'? Of course not, you are going to have to offer
something far more reassuring than that – platitudes will
not help when the dark night of the soul comes. What is
required is something far more comforting and uplifting.

It is the need to know the Truth. That is, to be enabled to begin to see things the way *God* sees things. That is precisely what this pastor, Peter, does for these Christians who feel very much at odds with a world that despises and rejects them. The way Peter reassures these beleaguered believers, and us, is to draw on the Old Testament imagery of the temple to present three glorious truths, all of which have God at the centre.

The Presence of God (vv. 4–5)

When you are being kicked around from pillar to post, as was happening to Christians at this time, with some already having been driven out of Rome, you are going to feel very insecure. What structure would convey a sense of overwhelming permanence and stability? One answer would be a great temple, like the one back in Jerusalem, or better still like the one Solomon the Great had built. Here was an architectural masterpiece, made from huge blocks of stone, 4 feet high and 15 feet long. 'Well', says Peter in effect, 'you are being built up into a temple, one which will eventually dwarf the temple in Jerusalem, one which will remain when that has been trampled into the dust', as happened in AD 70. 'For you, my brothers and sisters, are being made into a *spiritual* temple as you come to Jesus who is the chief cornerstone or capstone. As you are united to him, then you are being incorporated into this huge edifice being made in heaven – a spiritual house. All of this comes about when you come to Jesus through believing the Gospel – plain and simple.' The cornerstone was not only the first stone to be set in place, it actually constrained the rest of the building. It defined the angles of the walls, everything was aligned in relation to this stone. What is more, Peter

describes Jesus as the 'living Stone'. That is, he is alive
and now exists above all the ruling authorities which are
possibly giving Christians so much difficulty in the
world. *He* is immovable, solid, dependable and true. To
be sure, he was rejected by men, but he has been chosen
by God and is precious to him as he is precious to
Christians. In one sense Christians are not to be surprised if the same happens to them, the other living
stones. Just because they are having a rough time, this
does not mean that God has abandoned them any more
than he abandoned Jesus. On the contrary, rejection by
men is not a sign that we are rejected by God, for as he
is precious, we too are precious as we are united to him.

What is more, the temple symbolised the presence of
God, Yahweh dwelling in the midst of his people. There
could be no greater blessing than having the eternal God
with us; this is the supreme sign of blessing. It is in fact
a moving back to the original state in Eden, when God
and man walked and talked together in the garden. Man
was at peace with God, having a harmony totally unsullied by sin. After the Fall, the sign of God's curse is being
cast out of God's presence, as Adam was thrown out of
Eden. Here all that is being reversed. As we come to
Jesus, God comes to us.

Peter then extends the metaphor further by saying
that his readers are 'to be a holy priesthood offering spiritual sacrifices'. The point being made is that priests
were the only people who were allowed into God's presence in the temple. For everyone else, to dare to come
into the presence of God was to sign their own death
warrant. In order to overcome this, special folk were set
aside who had to obey strict rituals to enable them to
come into the inner sanctum to offer various sacrifices.
But now special priests are no longer required. Why?
Because a Christian believer is already a priest,

belonging to the holy priesthood of *all* believers. They have direct access into God's presence, anywhere and at any time.

Far from God abandoning Christians in persecution then, they cannot get any closer to him than they already are at this very moment. The God whose genius made the stars and galaxies and sent them spinning into space, the one who designed the constellations and the nebulas, the one who conceived and holds in being the DNA molecule, more than that, the very God whose voice thundered at Sinai and sent the Israelites cowering in fear – because it was a voice which terrified – this is the God who dwells in the believer and amongst his people as they gather. Certainly a church might not look very impressive as far as the world is concerned, meeting together in their houses or in a leaky old building, just as Jesus didn't look very impressive as he was hung on a Roman gibbet, but that is where God was making a special people for himself, laying the foundation-stone from which a human temple would be made, comprising of billions and billions of people, glistening with the translucent glory of God into all eternity.

The Provision of God (vv. 6–8)

How has this miracle of men and women being brought into God's presence been achieved?

Peter refers to three Old Testament passages that tell us how.

First, there is a quote from Isaiah 28:16. Here the prophet Isaiah is speaking to the rulers of Jerusalem who are so cocksure they are safe that nothing could touch them. Certainly the Northern tribes might be wiped out by the Assyrians, but it is inconceivable that those who live in Jerusalem, Mount Zion, with its holy temple, should be attacked. What do they do? They reject the preaching of the prophets like Jeremiah and Ezekiel and keep on thumbing their noses at God. They were good 'church going people', so they thought that nothing could ever upset them. In short, they were trusting in the wrong things – in their own religious heritage, their upbringing – and so they had a rude awakening when Jerusalem was finally sacked with the most unbelievable cruelty in 589 BC. Here, through the prophet God points them to where they *should* be putting their trust, in this person who was to come, a precious cornerstone. This is probably the background to Jesus saying 'On this rock [this stone] I will build my church and the gates of Hades will not overcome it.'

A few years ago a missionary working in Central America visited Britain and the United States and these were his impressions: 'The dominant feeling I get increasingly in western churches, is fear. People are afraid. They are afraid of what's going on in the culture. They are afraid of what is going on in society; they are afraid of the meaninglessness bound up with their young people; they are afraid of their own futures; and out of that fear they lash out. We are a frightened people and a frightened culture.' This is even more the case after the events of September 11th. But where are people going to put their trust? In the special forces rooting out the terrorists? In the latest soap opera to provide a way of escape? What about coming back to Jesus, whom God has provided and through whom we are adopted into God's family and made his children; one who offers a future beyond the grave, and his presence with us while living on earth?

Those who do come to him discover that he is precious (v. 7); but not everyone sees things that way. Peter quotes from Psalm 118 and then from Isaiah 8:7b:

> The stone the builders rejected
> has become the capstone,

and,

> A stone that causes men to stumble
> and a rock that makes them fall.

In other words, if we are not careful the living stone can become a tripping stone, and which one Jesus is to us depends upon how we respond to him. For those who see him as God's chief cornerstone or capstone, he provides security not only against the uncertainties of living in the present, but also from the judgement of God which is to come in the future. But if we reject him, seeing Jesus as having no more significance than, say, a stone which has been discarded and is laying around the builder's yard, then we had better watch out for we will trip over him and fall headlong into perdition. That is the picture Peter is presenting us with. This is not something that is accidental, it is a deliberate choice on our part, those who '*disobey* the message'. If we refuse to believe the Gospel then our destiny will be condemnation, 'what we are destined *for*'. Everything worthwhile turns on our response to the Gospel.

The Praise of God (vv. 9–12)

Peter has Exodus 19 in mind and the choosing of Israel to be a royal priesthood, a holy nation, a people belonging to God. The danger of being referred to as a 'chosen people' is that it causes us to focus on all the privileges we have, as if we are special and so to be pampered. Certainly there are the most tremendous privileges of knowing God personally and being called by name, but the focus is more on the responsibilities Christians have. Like Israel, the people of the New Covenant have been chosen for a purpose, namely 'to declare the praises of him who called you out of darkness into his wonderful light' (v. 9). People who have received mercy are to declare to others God's mercy.

That declaration is two-fold.

There is the praise of our *lips*. Although it is worship language that Peter is using here – 'praise' – and of course the temple was the place par excellence where the praise of God's people was heard as they sang psalms – as we shall see elsewhere, in the New Testament such language is extended to include the *whole* of the Christian life. So, for example, the apostle Paul in Romans 15:16 speaks of his evangelism as being his priestly duty, the offering up of Gentile converts as sacrificial fruit offerings to God. This declaring God's praise out of sheer gratitude for what he has done for us in saving us – bringing us out of darkness into the splendid light of the Gospel – involves sharing our faith, as Peter goes on to explain a little more fully in chapter 3. Today worship has been too narrowly defined as simply praise; actually it is much bigger than that and includes evangelism.

But as well as declaring his praise with our lips we are also to do it with our *lives*: 'Live such good lives among the pagans that, though they accuse you of doing wrong, they may see your good deeds and glorify God on the day he visits us.' Christians are different, they do not belong to this world-order, which is in constant rebellion against its Maker, but to a 'New World-order' which acknowledges Jesus as the rightful ruler. Consequently their lives are to reflect that. The point Peter is making is simple and profound: though people may not like what

Christians believe, they should not be able to fault the way they behave. That doesn't mean that Christians are perfect, but rather that there should be a consistency and integrity forged between belief and behaviour in such a way that folk will say, 'You know, although I can't go in for all this believing in Jesus nonsense, you have to give it to these Christians, they are at least honest – you can trust them and they do work hard, their lifestyle is simple and not as materialistic as the rest of us. They genuinely seem content. I hate to admit it, but I do wish I had what they have.' When will they do that? 'On a day [the Greek does not have a definite article] God visits us.' This phrase occurs nowhere else in the Bible. It is open-ended, simply speaking of a time, which could be repeated, when God visits his people in either blessing or judgement. So as God is at work in and through his church, some of the people who are presently slandering Christians become converted and in this sense 'glorify God'. They may begin by resisting, but because of what they see and hear, end up believing. The process may be long and drawn out but the end is sure. What an encouragement to get on with Christian witness!

A few years ago a survey was carried out amongst Christians in Britain to find out what it was that led them to follow Christ in the first place. What was found was most interesting. It was discovered first of all that for 27.8 per cent it was the influence of a particular church over a period of time. The second greatest factor at 25.8 per cent was the influence of other members of one's own family. Third, at 19.9 per cent the influence of a Christian friend or friends, and at the bottom of the list at 13.2 per cent it was a specific evangelistic activity. These findings simply go to show that what Peter is saying here is so perceptive – the way in which people give glory to God is by the regular, day-to-day witness of ordinary Christians.

How do many Christians feel today in the west? Often as a despised, misunderstood minority. Peter calls us to think again, '*for you* are a chosen people, a royal priesthood, a holy nation, a people belonging to God so you may declare the praises of him who called you out of darkness into his wonderful light'.

3

The Marks of the Church
Acts 2:42–7

They devoted themselves to the apostles' teaching and to the fellowship, to the breaking of bread and to prayer. Everyone was filled with awe, and many wonders and miraculous signs were done by the apostles. All the believers were together and had everything in common. Selling their possessions and goods, they gave to anyone as he had need. Every day they continued to meet together in the temple courts. They broke bread in their homes and ate together with glad and sincere hearts, praising God and enjoying the favor of all the people. And the Lord added to their number daily those who were being saved.

A few years ago a brochure was circulated inviting ministers to a huge conference called the 'Gathering of Champions'. They were told that at this conference thousands of people would gather together to hear some of the most powerful speakers in the world. One pastor was an exemplary lyricist and composer, his songs would reach and touch the soul and had earned him a Grammy award. He was also Senior Pastor of the Perfecting Church that consists of 2,900 members. There would also be another powerful speaker there whose church is 18,000 strong, along with a pastor who runs a church called the Winners' Chapel claiming to attract 40,000. The ministries of these men, it was said, are concerned with challenging people to live lives that lead to success and prosperity. A financial breakthrough was assured. A further pastor had written over 5,000 songs and 57 books. It sounds so great! Churches of thousands, success and prosperity all the way! Who can resist that?

But it raises the question: just what are the marks of an authentic church? Is it all about numbers and success, or is it something else? A pastor of a church in Washington DC in America has gone on record in saying the size of the church car park is the mark of success in the States. He was slightly worried because he didn't have one! However, when we come to the New Testament we discover that God's criteria for success are entirely different. Success is measured in terms of faithfulness, doctrinal orthodoxy, obedience to Jesus' commands and love for one another. They cannot be measured in numbers and figures, but they tell the true story about the health of a church. And that is the question we are concerned with in this chapter. What are the marks of the true church of God?

The answer to that question is found by looking at the earliest Christian church, that gathering of people in Jerusalem who met in the days after Jesus had ascended to heaven. In the passage from Acts 2, Luke is explaining just what that church did. It is a little cameo of those first gatherings. But before we look in greater detail at the marks of that church, we need to pause and see just who was in it. As has been reiterated throughout this book, the 'church' in the Bible is simply another way of saying a 'gathering of believers'. Church equals people, not buildings. The church building is simply a rain-shelter under which the real church, the people of God, meet. Luke tells us what kind of people they were in verses 38–41. Peter is giving his first sermon all about Jesus, and it is not a bad effort. The effects of this sermon are that three thousand people repent of their sins, accept the message about Jesus and receive the gift of the Holy Spirit! They are new believers. In the next verses Luke tells us that these are the folk who met together daily.

So what was this church like? What were the things that characterised this newly Spirit-filled people of God?

A Learning Church

The first mark of this church that we discover in verse 42 is that it was a *learning church*. They were devoted, says Luke, to the 'apostles' teaching'. The teaching of the apostles was something that captivated them. They were like newborn babies desperate to get at the food that their spiritual fathers were giving them. What exactly was this teaching of the apostles? Judging by their letters in the New Testament, it was teaching about Jesus, who he was, what he came to do, how to obey him, and his second coming. In other words, the *whole* Christian faith. These first Christians were devoted to that teaching. The word Luke uses is a very strong word: they had a 'hunger' for the Word of God as taught by the apostles. It was the apostles' teaching because they were the divinely accredited witnesses of Jesus. That is why Luke records that the apostles did many signs and wonders in the midst of the people. The miracles were divine signposts that something amazing was happening, and that these men should be listened to. As the writer John Stott says: 'The Spirit of God leads the people of God to submit to the Word of God.'

The great thing is that we are in exactly the same position. God in his goodness has left us with copies of those first amazing adult Bible classes. It is called the New Testament. We have in our hands, free and available the teaching of the apostles, Jesus' spokesmen. A church which is a healthy church will want to make the teaching of the Bible one of its primary tasks. Any church which does not do that, and is not built on the teaching of the Bible will be a sick church. Christians will not be fed, non-Christians will not hear the gospel, and that church will eventually die. Sadly that is happening all over Britain. Where the Word of God is not taught, the people of God starve.

But, of course, the danger is that we could easily say, 'Well, we've got the first box ticked. Let's move on to the next. Let's pat ourselves on the back and say, well done. We do devote ourselves to Scripture.' But there is a further application to ourselves, because it was the individuals who made up that first gathering who were devoted to the teaching of the apostles. It requires each of us to ask ourselves personally, 'Am I similarly devoted?' All right, we may go to the home groups and hear the sermons every week, but what about the rest of the week? Am I devoted to the Word of God, do I hunger for it like these first Christians? That is much more challenging. Statistics about the decline in personal daily Bible reading are horrifying. A good test is to add up honestly how much TV you watch each week, and then compare it with your Bible reading. It may be an eye-opening exercise! It's not that TV is bad in itself, but we must ask ourselves, 'Whose message are we receiving more, the world's or God's?' Who is shaping our moral decisions? Kilroy or Christ? It's not surprising that biblical morality and doctrine get pushed to the side, even among Christians, when God's Word is sidelined.

It was said of John Bunyan that if you cut him open anywhere you would discover that his blood was 'bibline'. He devoted himself to reading Scripture. That devotion is to be ours as well. If there's room for 'Coronation Street', there's room for the Bible.

A Caring Church

Luke tells us that the second mark of this church was that it was a caring church. They had a desire to love others. In verse 42, Luke points out that they devoted themselves to the 'fellowship'. This is perhaps one of the most misunderstood words in Bible vocabulary. If you invite a non-Christian friend round for a cup of tea at your house, you are doing evangelism, we're told. But if you invite a Christian friend round for tea, then it's fellowship! But the word 'fellowship' (*koinonia*) actually means far more than that. At its root it simply means partnership or sharing, so Luke is able to use a related word to describe the fishing business that Andrew and John had with Peter. They were partners in 'Zebedee and Sons Fishing Company Ltd'. John uses the same word in his first letter to describe the relationship between the Christian and God. It is fellowship, a deep personal commitment, which is a loving relationship and spiritual union. But it also means something intensely practical. That is why Paul can talk about the Macedonian church's willingness to give to the famine-stricken Jerusalem church as 'fellowship' in 2 Corinthians 8. So fellowship is much more than sipping tea. It is a deep, personal commitment that is intensely practical. That is precisely what this first church in Acts 2 demonstrated.

Verses 44–5 spell this out for us: 'All the believers were together and had everything in common. Selling their possessions and goods, they gave to anyone as they had need.' The big question that is always raised is: should we do the same? Should all of us sell everything and all live together in the vicarage or manse in one large commune? It is unlikely that that is a fair application of the passage.

To begin with, it is clear that not everyone sold everything. They clearly still had homes to meet in where they broke bread, and in Acts 4 we discover that Barnabas still had a field to sell. Then, in verse 34, Luke tells us that 'from time to time those who owned lands or houses sold them, brought the money from the sales and laid it at the apostles' feet. It is quite clear that the selling of property was a continuous thing as and when the need arose. They didn't just sell everything and live together. It would have been impractical with over three thousand of them! Furthermore, in Acts 5 when we read the story of Ananias and Sapphira, we see that their sin was not greed, but deceit. Peter himself says to them that they are free to do what they want with their property. Their sin was to lie to God.

What becomes clear is that this church's fellowship was seen in their willingness not to have any needy persons among them. They were so generous that they willingly gave up their own things for the sake of others. They treated their own possessions as if they belonged to others. There was no selfish accumulation of goods whilst a fellow brother or sister was in need. The Spirit of God led them to be intensely generous and caring for one another.

Even if we can explain away some interpretations of this passage, we must be very careful not to water down the force of the challenge. Their generosity and costly love for one another often puts us to shame when we western twenty-first century Christians are so individualistic and materialistic. It certainly makes us ask big questions about our attitudes to possessions and money. It is highly doubtful that many of these people were very wealthy. And yet they were willing to say 'What is mine is yours.' In our terms it is like saying: 'I don't need my car this weekend, why not take it for a day out with the family. I'll pay the insurance.' 'Your husband is in hospital, why not come round for a meal and we'll take you to see him.' Or take our regular giving. Barnabas was able to sell a field, a valuable asset, for the sake of the church fellowship. What about selling something for the sake of the local church's work so that the gospel can be spread further abroad? When you bank with heaven, the returns are excellent. Not everyone will be able to give vast amounts financially. Generosity is seen in other ways as well: in time, care, concern. The point here is to take the challenge of these first Christians. They genuinely cared for one another. It was a mark of the Spirit of God among them that they loved one another.

Many people have heard of Chuck Colson. He was one of President Nixon's top advisors in the USA in the 1970s. As a result of his complicity in the Watergate crisis, Chuck Colson was put in prison. Colson had become a Christian before he went into prison, and yet it was still an extremely difficult time for him – his wife did not understand, his son was charged for drugs offences and he was getting depressed. But one old senator, a man called Senator Quie, who was also a Christian, discovered an old law which said that someone could step into the shoes of the criminal and take their place in jail. So Senator Quie offered to take Colson's place in jail and serve the rest of the sentence. Senator Quie put his love into action. He was willing to go to jail for his Christian brother. That's the sort of love which these Christians were showing. A healthy church will be a caring church.

A Committed Church

Caring arises out of commitment to God, the Gospel and one another, verse 46: 'Every day they continued to meet together in the temple courts. They broke bread in their homes and ate together with glad and sincere hearts, praising God and enjoying the favour of all the people.' This was a *very* committed church. They met together daily in those early days. Their meetings were both formal and informal. They were formal in the sense that they continued to meet together at the temple. They would use the daily meetings there as a focus for their own meetings, even though as time went on the Christians would see the radical break with Judaism that was needed. Jesus was the fulfilment of all that had gone before. It was also informal in that they met together in their homes. There we are told they broke bread, probably a reference to an early form of the Lord's supper. It is likely that they would have shared a meal together and it would naturally have moved on to a time of remembering Jesus' work on the cross and rejoicing in the good things that Christ had done for them. It was a time of both joy and sincerity and they found that they were attractive to the outside world. A church that is committed to the Gospel and to one another will be attractive to outsiders. It will be clear that there is something different about these folk. And Luke also tells us in verse 42 that a vital ingredient of these meetings was prayer. They were 'devoted to prayer'.

What was not in doubt was their commitment. You can't imagine them having a debate about whether to meet with their fellow brothers and sisters or to stay in and to watch 'Gladiators 'on TV! They were 100 per cent committed. In an age when commitment is itself seen to be passé this comes as a big challenge. Our commitment as Christians to meet together and to pray together is to be wholehearted.

When we see that the church is a gathering of fellow believers who need our support and encouragement week by week, then we'll see just how important it is to keep meeting together. Because we need their support too. Even your very presence is an encouragement to the rest of the body. We should never gather as church thinking 'What's the point?' for we all have a job to do. These early Christians saw that, and they met joyfully and gladly.

Emperor penguins live in the Antarctic and the temperature there gets as low as minus 40 degrees Celsius, and for much of the year the sun doesn't shine. How do Emperor penguins survive? During the dark season, which lasts for several months, they all stand in a huge circle close together. The penguins on the edge of the circle get very cold, so they keep moving round, so when you have done your stint on the outer ring, you move to the warmth of the inner circle. They do this for months on end, living off their fat reserves until the sun shines again. Now imagine if you were a rather rebellious Emperor penguin and didn't want to spend time with these other penguins. So you came and went as you pleased and decided to try and make it through the winter on your own. The trouble is, of course, you would eventually die without the support and warmth of the other penguins. And it's the same for the Christian. We need the encouragement of one another to keep going. We need to be committed for our own sakes and for the sake of fellow Christians in the church. That is exactly how this first church was.

A Growing Church

Not surprisingly with all of these characteristics being expressed, they were a growing church. Verse 47: 'And

the Lord added to their number daily those who were
being saved.' We are to notice who does the growing. It
is the Lord. He is the one who is building his church, and
he is the one who will bring people into it. But it is also
clear from Acts that this first church was actively
involved in mission. Its people didn't just sit back and
expect God to do the saving. Mission was at the very
heart of this first church. These people had a passion for
the lost. It was not an added extra, either, something that
they were forced to do by a manipulative pastor. Rather
it was natural part of their new found delight in being
saved by God. In Jesus they had met the Saviour and
King and they longed for others to hear that same message.

In any healthy church, the spreading of the gospel
will be at the heart, shaping its activities, its prayers and
its priorities. That's why we should always be thinking
of ways to tell others, and that's why we should always
be thinking of expanding. Not because we are in the
numbers game, but because we are prayerfully expect-
ing God to increase our number as more people are
saved. That's why church planting should not be for the
special big churches, but something every church can be
doing at the right time and in the right ways. We'll be
always looking around us to see what areas of our community need special input, where it may be good to start
some evangelistic initiative. We will also be praying for
opportunities ourselves and playing our part, however
small. It was Archbishop William Temple who said
that the church was the only club designed for its non-
members. He was absolutely right. These people saw
that and so the church grew.

What are the marks of a healthy church? Is it large
congregations of thousands, is it huge car parks, and
impressive buildings, is it slick pastors who churn out

books and hymns at a fast rate of knots? When we look at the New Testament, the answer is no. Rather a healthy church is a learning church, where the people hunger for the Word of God, a caring church, where our desire is to love others, a committed church, where our commitment is to meet together, and a growing church, where we have a passion for the lost. Do you want to belong to a church like that? Maybe you belong to one already? If so thank God. But there is always room for improvement.

4

The Calling of the Church
Ephesians 1:1–14

Paul, an apostle of Christ Jesus by the will of God,

To the saints in Ephesus, the faithful in Christ Jesus:

Grace and peace to you from God our Father and the Lord Jesus Christ.

Praise be to the God and Father of our Lord Jesus Christ, who has blessed us in the heavenly realms with every spiritual blessing in Christ. For he chose us in him before the creation of the world to be holy and blameless in his sight. In love he predestined us to be adopted as his sons through Jesus Christ, in accordance with his pleasure and will – to the praise of his glorious grace, which he has freely given us in the One he loves. In him we have redemption through his blood, the forgiveness of sins, in accordance with the riches of God's grace that he lavished on us with all wisdom and understanding. And he made known to us the mystery of his will according to his good pleasure, which he purposed in Christ, to be put into effect when the times will have reached their fulfillment – to bring all things in heaven and on earth together under one head, even Christ.

In him we were also chosen, having been predestined according to the plan of him who works out everything in conformity with the purpose of his will, in order that we, who were the first to hope in Christ, might be for the praise of his glory. And you also were included in Christ when you heard the word of truth, the gospel of your salvation. Having believed, you were marked in him with a seal, the promised Holy Spirit, who is a deposit guaranteeing our inheritance until the redemption of those who are God's possession – to the praise of his glory.

For this reason, ever since I heard about your faith in the Lord Jesus and your love for all the saints, I have not stopped giving thanks for you, remembering you in my prayers. I keep asking that the God of our Lord Jesus Christ, the glorious Father, may give you the Spirit of wisdom and revelation, so that you may know him better. I pray also that the eyes of your heart may be enlightened in order that you may know the hope to which he has called you, the riches of his glorious inheritance in the saints, and his incomparably great power for us who believe. That power is like the working of his mighty strength, which he exerted in Christ when he raised him from the dead and seated him at his right hand in the heavenly realms, far above all rule and authority, power and dominion, and every title that can be given, not only in the present age but also in the one to come. And God placed all things under his feet and appointed him to be head over everything for the church, which is his body, the fullness of him who fills everything in every way.

Here are some penetrating words written by the Christian missionary speaker Michael Griffiths:

Christians collectively seem to be suffering from a strange amnesia. A high proportion of people who 'go to

church' have forgotten what it is for. Week by week they
attend services in a special building and go through their
particular, time-honoured routine, but give little thought
to the purpose of what they are doing . . . The Bible talks
about 'the bride of Christ', but the church today seems
like a ragged Cinderella, hideous among the ashes. She
has forgotten that she is supposed to be growing up, as
the soap advertisements used to have it, 'to be a beautiful lady'! Many Christians can rattle off glibly the
various biblical pictures of the church as 'building', and
'body' and 'bride' but in their experience these ideas
have never got beyond a theoretical stage, and they continue to be disappointed with, and disillusioned by, the
church as they know it'.

It is perhaps significant that Griffiths called his book
from which those words are taken, *Cinderella with
Amnesia*. When you think about it, that is an accurate
description of the way many churches operate. While
the church is in fact a princess, the bride of the King of
glory, destined to be the most dazzling and beautiful
entity in the whole universe, the picture we conceive of
ourselves and convey to others is that of an abandoned
orphan, sitting by the fire grate amongst the cinders,
looking puzzlingly at a glass slipper that seems to
suggest that we should be much more, but not quite
knowing what.

A passage that is guaranteed to snap us out of our
spiritual amnesia and remind us once again of just who
we are and where we are heading as the people of God
is Ephesians 1:1–14.

As we have seen the word 'church', *ekklesia*, from
which we derive the term 'ecclesiastical', simply means
'a gathering'. When the term is used in the New
Testament to describe Christians gathering it almost

always has two gatherings primarily in mind – the gathering of Christ's people around his throne in heaven, and the smaller gatherings of his people on earth – local churches. Each local church is meant to reflect, and be a preparation for, the heavenly church. Just as an overhead projector projects onto a screen the figure on an acetate, so the local church is to project into the world something of the perfected and glorified church that is now rejoicing in glory. The very life of heaven is meant to pulsate through Christians as they meet!

However, a gathering or a congregation doesn't just happen to come together by chance; it is *called* into being by God with a specific purpose in mind. Indeed, this is suggested by the Greek word for church. *Ekklesia* is linked to the verb *ek-kaleo* – to be called out. The call, calling and the church are intrinsically related to each other. In Ephesians 3:21 we read these words: 'To him be glory in the church and in Christ Jesus throughout all generations, for ever and ever. Amen.' And then straight away, in chapter 4:1, Paul goes on to write: 'Therefore, I urge you to live a life worthy of the *calling* you have received.' It could be translated something like this: 'Walk worthy of the churching by which you have been churched.'

Just what the calling together of Christians as a church involves is spelt out for us in Ephesians 1.

In the original this is one long sentence. Everything flows from those opening words of praise and adoration in verse 3: 'Praise be to the God and Father of our Lord Jesus Christ, who has blessed us in the heavenly realms with every spiritual blessing in Christ.' What a way to begin a letter! Here we are told quite plainly that the church is anything but a 'Cinderella', although that is what we may look like to the world. Rather, the church is a princess who has all the promised spiritual treasures of her adoring groom just waiting for her. We are to notice too that in the original Paul uses the plural when he speaks of 'you'. We tend to read this letter as if it is addressing us individually when in fact it is speaking to a collective group of people who *together* are the recipients of all of God's gracious love. So verse 1: 'To the *saints* in Ephesus, the *faithful* in Christ Jesus.' Paul talks about 'us' and 'you' in the plural. There is no such thing as a Lone Ranger Christian, going it alone, just me and Jesus (Even the Lone Ranger had Tonto!). We are in this together, as we are called together.

How does this calling take place? It involves four aspects of divine action.

The Church's Election

Paul tells us that we are *called before*. 'For he chose us in him *before* the creation of the world' (v. 4a). 'In love he *predestined* us to be adopted as his sons through Jesus Christ, in accordance with his pleasure and will' (v. 5). 'In him we were chosen, having been *predestined* according to the plan of him who works out everything in conformity with the purpose of his will' (v. 11). The gathering together of a special people was not some afterthought for God. It was in his heart even before the dawn of the time. We are to notice three things about this choosing by God.

First, this choosing is *personal* – '*He* chose *us in* Christ.' We are not faceless numbers to him, each of our names is engraved on the palm of his hands. As a parent chooses specific boys and girls to be adopted into the family, so our Father God chose us to belong to his family; we are known to him and we matter to him.

Secondly, this choosing is *unconditional* – 'in accordance with *his pleasure and will*'. God did not choose

Melvin Tinker or Nathan Buttery because they were particularly nice fellows or because he foresaw that they
had bags of potential and were bound to make fantastic
ministers some day! It was simply his will and good
pleasure to look upon them in his tender love and save
them. He simply wanted to. Isn't that amazing?

Thirdly, this choosing is *successful*. He has a plan for
his people and because he is the all-knowing and
all-wise God, he is able to 'work out *everything* in conformity with the purpose of his will'. Everything? That
is what the text says. A moment's reflection soon reveals
why it has to be everything. If God is going to satisfy the
eternal longing of his heart in gathering around his
throne in heaven a family devoted to his Son, then he
cannot afford to be taken by surprise, for then he would
run the risk of failure, losing one of his children and so
ending up with an incomplete church. Since we live in a
world where everything is interconnected with everything else, then God has to superintend *all* events, great
and small, weaving them into a pattern and direction
which will result in every single one of his children making it to their true heavenly home. God was not, therefore, taken by surprise with the rage of men like Nero,
Hitler, Stalin or Pol Pot as they sought to obliterate his
people. God is not taken by surprise with that change in
our personal circumstances either, with that particular
illness, or that loss of a job, or the failure of that exam
which meant so much to us. God will use even these to
shape us and clean us up, getting his bride ready for the
great wedding day. Our calling began in eternity and
will take us into eternity. That is meant to be a comforting thought. That is the sort of belief we need to hold on
to when life throws up all sorts of nasty surprises and
disappointments, to know that God has so fixed his love
upon us, that nothing can ever shake it off.

The Church's Redemption

In the second place, we are *called out*. 'In him we have redemption through his blood, the forgiveness of sins' (v. 7). The film *Schindler's List* must be one of the most harrowing and powerful films ever made. It tells of a German businessman, Oscar Schindler and his attempt to rescue Jews from the Nazi concentration camps. Towards the end of the film, there is a moving scene in which Schindler can do no more. He has given so much of his genius, his money, his very self simply to rescue these people from the most wretched nightmare imaginable. At this point he simply breaks down and cries, 'But here I have a ring, maybe this could have been used to buy one more soul.' By that one man's action hundreds were taken out of a living hell into freedom. Do we need to be reminded what price God has paid for our freedom, so we can be saved from a literal hell?' Yes we do; that is why Christians celebrate the Lord's Supper, reminding them that they are saved by his 'blood'; not with gold rings or bribes as in the case of Schindler, but by a single man hanging on a Roman gallows in our place to free us from our sin in order to take us out of a world immersed in darkness and moral corruption and into a new spiritual dimension filled with light and goodness. All that happens by believing a message and receiving a Spirit: 'And you were included in Christ when you *heard* the word of truth, the Gospel of your salvation. Having *believed*, you were *marked* in him with a seal, the promised Holy Spirit' (v. 13).

There is something very special about sharing a common experience. It forms a common bond between people. Think of reunions like those of war veterans. In theory non-veterans could be invited along as guests, but they would feel quite out of place no matter how friendly the others might be. Why? Because they have not been through what the veterans have experienced. For one thing, many of them came face to face with death and survived, and they are grateful. There are many people who attend a church week after week and still do not feel a part. It is not necessarily because folk aren't friendly nor is it because there are class or cultural differences (although those may be real factors). The main reason may well be that they are those who have not yet personally responded to this message, who have not yet seen themselves as lost, unworthy and in need of a loving Saviour. But when they do and ask Christ to forgive them and come in and make his home with them by his Spirit, then almost by magic, they feel one with the rest of the family.

The Church's Identification

When that happens people see what they are *called to*. 'For he chose us in him before the creation of the world *to be holy and blameless in his sight*' (v. 4). 'You were included *in* Christ' (v. 13). The church is intimately identified with its Lord, the risen and ascended Jesus. Notice that for Paul it is all a matter of being 'in' Christ or 'with' Christ, which means becoming more and more 'like Christ' – holy and blameless. This in fact takes us to the heart of what being church is all about. It is a love relationship. The picture Paul uses in chapter 5 of the church being the bride of Christ underscores this.

You may have noticed that those who start to fall in love, soon begin, often unconsciously, to mimic each other. They find themselves mirroring the other's movements. She leans forward over her coffee cup, so does he. She is interested in ballet, and now, miraculously, so is he, although a few minutes earlier he couldn't tell *The Nutcracker* from *Swan Lake*! And of course in marriage itself, the unity enters a new dimension, two become 'one flesh' and we have – to use a modern term – an item. Likewise, the church gathering is an 'item' with the Lord Jesus. He has infused his very life and soul into his people by his Spirit, so that with the passage of time his likes become their likes, his concerns their concerns. Certainly, like any relationship it has to be worked at, old habits have to be replaced with new ones, but as the love is kept fresh the understanding develops and bit by bit the church begins to reflect the life of Jesus himself, and exhibits the family likeness.

The Unification of the Church

Which brings us on to the next aspect of our calling, we are *called with*. Paul says that God's will is to 'bring all things in heaven and on earth *together* under one head, even Christ' (v. 10). That is the goal of redemption history and the church is meant to be a symbol of that future now. The local church is to reflect the unity and community of the heavenly church and so display before the watching world that there is a better way.

We live in a society that is increasingly fragmented and isolating. Even the community offered by work now seems to be under threat as with high tech computers, Internet and cell phones, people tend to work alone at home or simply travel around from one place to another. Our society is becoming soulless, with more and more lonely people. Where are people to look to see what real community is if not the local church? This is the way Charles Colson puts it: 'The church is no civic center, no social club or encounter group, no Sunday

morning meeting place. It is a new society, created for
the salvation of a lost world, pointing to the kingdom to
come.' That is why churches need to create opportunities for their members to meet together, work together,
pray together, share together and give financially
together to show that the church is in the world to win
the world, and so allowing people to taste on earth what
can be fully enjoyed in heaven.

The Proclamation of the Church

Which brings us to our final calling, we are *called for*. 'To
the praise of his glory' (v. 12). We have been called to
proclaim the glory of God's grace, his undeserving, saving love. People should be able to point to us and say,
'Look at these people, what a God they have, look at
how he is working amongst them and through them!'
God should be glorified in how we live and what we say
as a fellowship.

At the end of time when all his people are gathered in,
then the whole world will praise God for what he has
done, and the angels will be caught up in that too. But it
should be going on now. Every time we pray the Lord's
prayer and say 'Hallowed or honoured be your name',
we are committing ourselves afresh to proclamation, so
that people will get to know this God and so honour him
as they submit their lives to his beloved Son. Howard
Snyder in his paper for the Lausanne Congress on World
Evangelization in 1974 wrote these words:

> The church is the only divinely appointed means for
> spreading the gospel . . . Further, evangelism makes lit-
> tle sense divorced from the fact of Christian community
> . . . The evangelistic call intends to call persons to the

Body of Christ. Biblical evangelism is church-centred evangelism. Evangelism should spark church growth, and the life and witness of the church should produce evangelism. In this sense the church is both the agent and the goal of evangelism.

This is our calling. The God of the universe has called us to this. The God of the cross died for this. The God of the resurrection sent his Spirit to enable this. The question is: will more and more churches respond?

5

Building Up the Church
Ephesians 4:1–16

As a prisoner for the Lord, then, I urge you to live a life worthy of the calling you have received. Be completely humble and gentle; be patient, bearing with one another in love. Make every effort to keep the unity of the Spirit through the bond of peace. There is one body and one Spirit – just as you were called to one hope when you were called – one Lord, one faith, one baptism; one God and Father of all, who is over all and through all and in all.

But to each one of us grace has been given as Christ apportioned it. This is why it says:

> *'When he ascended on high,*
> *he led captives in his train*
> *and gave gifts to men.'*

(What does 'he ascended' mean except that he also descended to the lower, earthly regions? He who descended is the very one who ascended higher than all the heavens, in order to fill the whole universe.) It was he who gave some to be apostles, some to be prophets, some to be evangelists, and some to be

*pastors and teachers, to prepare God's people for works of serv-
ice, so that the body of Christ may be built up until we all
reach unity in the faith and in the knowledge of the Son of God
and become mature, attaining to the whole measure of the fullness of Christ.*

*Then we will no longer be infants, tossed back and forth by
the waves, and blown here and there by every wind of teaching
and by the cunning and craftiness of men in their deceitful
scheming. Instead, speaking the truth in love, we will in all
things grow up into him who is the Head, that is, Christ. From
him the whole body, joined and held together by every supporting ligament, grows and builds itself up in love, as each
part does its work.*

Have you ever wondered what it would be like to be
marooned on a desert island all by yourself? I guess for
many of us the idea sounds wonderful: all that sea,
beautiful sand, fresh fruit to eat plucked from the trees
and plants, wonderful scenery, and above all . . . time.
Time to think and relax and enjoy your own company
without the hassle of everyday life. That romantic ideal
has been smashed to pieces in the Tom Hanks' movie,
Cast Away. In the film, Tom Hanks plays a man who is
washed up on a remote Pacific island after a plane crash.
He is completely isolated with very little food, no mod
cons and no way of escape. Much of the film shows the
man alone on the island, desperately trying to survive
against the odds, even to the point of doing some DIY
dentistry with an ice skate! If you dream of spending
your days on a desert island, then you need to watch the
film. It brings you back down to earth with a bump.

Coming from watching that film, one cannot help
thinking that the possibility was actually reality: that
many people are actually living castaway lives, even in
the middle of big cities. It's no secret that our society is

becoming ever more individualistic, as nuclear families become nuclear individuals. Thirty per cent of people now live on their own, and we exist in isolated little units, with our own close-knit circles of friends, living in closely guarded houses. The irony is that as the world gets smaller, the people get more insular and independent. The Tube in London is a classic example. If you were to travel on the Tube frequently, even on a long journey, it would be very surprising if anyone spoke to you at all, except to ask for money. Truly, we are living on our own islands, without the sea and sand, but just as isolated and lonely.

It is very easy for Christians to act the same, to be castaway Christians. The danger is that we simply turn up on a Sunday once a week to a gathering of individuals, sing a few songs, have some coffee and then go back to our homes and meet up a week later. The danger is that we become a church in name, but not in action. But that is not the way that God wants it. Rather, God is building for himself a new society, a people built together on the foundation of his Son, a people who are united under one Lord and who exist together and work together for the spreading of his Gospel. This people is the church.

It is these truths that Paul underscores in Ephesians 4: that Christians are a body, a body beautiful no less, a fully working, caring, moving body, all devoted to the same task, but all doing different jobs. That is a message we desperately need to hear. For we are to be counter-cultural, letting God's Word shape our minds and actions, living as the people of God are meant to live, not becoming more isolated, but growing more together. Here Paul tells us to be who we are and what we are meant to be. If we are the people of God, called by God, then we're to act as the people of God. What he says revolves around three vital issues.

The Church's Unity (vv. 1–6)

Before we immediately leap to thinking about church unity and the denominational unity that many people work for, we need to remember that this is not what Paul is addressing here. He is addressing a local church and talking about *their* unity. If Paul were here today in person, he would be saying exactly the same things to any local church as he did to the Ephesians. It is possible these verses have a secondary application to unity beyond the local church, but the focus is the local congregation.

He begins by talking about the *character of our unity*. Its character is loving. Verse 2: 'Be completely humble and gentle; be patient, bearing with one another in love.' This, says Paul, is what it means to live a life worthy of the calling you have received. Paul doesn't start with structures, he starts with love. We're to be completely humble, to put others first, and to be willing to play second fiddle. The church is not the place for showing ourselves off or for climbing over others to get to the top. Rather we are humbly to recognise the values and strengths and concerns of other people. We are to be gentle with others, not putting others down, but being gracious with them. We are to be patient, bearing with one another in love. How easy it is to get short with others, to find fault in them and to become irritated with one another, forgetting the planks in our own eyes, when we see the specks in those of others. Did you notice that all these things could be said of Jesus? He was the model par excellence of humility, gentleness, patience and love. He placed others' needs above his own, considering others' needs more important than his own.

It is obvious that a church which is founded on those principles will be able to maintain its unity and togetherness. The Christians will be prepared to let things happen which they may not like but which they know others want and which are for the good of the church. They will be willing to lay aside their own small hang-ups for the sake of others, be they theological or otherwise. But what happens when petty jealousy and rivalries take over? If you reverse these qualities what do you get? Pride instead of humility, bitterness instead of gentleness, sharp tongues instead of patience, hatred instead of love. How often do we see that in churches? Churches are more often than not split from the inside out, rather than from the outside in!

Robert Louis Stevenson tells the story of two unmarried sisters who shared a single room. As people who live in close quarters are apt to do, they fell out. The dispute was over a theological issue. The trouble was that the dispute was so intense that they didn't agree to differ, they simply didn't speak to each other, ever again. It became so bad that the two sisters drew a line with chalk down the middle of their room to mark off their respective territories. They continued to live in the same room together, but never said a word as long as they lived. Each one endured the silence of the other as friends came round or they ate meals. In this way, the two sisters lived out the rest of their miserable lives together. Pride and selfishness are so often at the root of disunity, and if a gathering of Christians are to grow together as a church, then these loving qualities will have to be at the very heart of all they do. And that will be costly. Putting ourselves second and loving others first is always hard, but it must be the character of our unity.

Paul doesn't leave it there. He goes on to teach us *the grounds of our unity*. A church is not just a bunch of people who love one another because they support a particular football club, or spot trains; rather the unity is based in the *Gospel*. Verse 4: 'There is one body and one Spirit, just as you were called to one hope when you were called, one Lord, one faith [probably referring to the Gospel itself as opposed to our belief in it], one baptism; one God and Father who is over all and through all and in all.' Notice that this Gospel is rooted in the Father and the Son (who is the Lord) and the Spirit. Since there is only one God, then there can only be one faith. Also there can only be one baptism, the marker of those who come to him. What is more there can only be one hope, and for this reason there can only be one body, his church. Paul is thinking here of that universal heavenly gathering around the throne of heaven, of which each local church is an earthly manifestation.

This is the Gospel professing Christians have come to believe and accept. It is the grounds of their unity. This means that if someone who claims to be a Christian does not hold to these fundamental truths of the Gospel, then we cannot by definition be united with them. They believe something else. By all means we should dialogue with them, but let us not term it unity. For it is the Gospel that is to be the bedrock on which Christ builds his church, made up of those who confess this truth. Christians are a people born again through the Spirit, and so they have a God-given unity in the truth. But notice what Paul says in verse 3: 'Make every effort to keep the unity of the Spirit.' Unity is not something we have to make up. We have it through the Spirit in the Gospel. Since we have such Gospel unity, we need to keep it that way. That, says Paul, will mean the hard work of being loving and humble. Each Christian has experienced something precious in the saving work of God, so, says Paul, make sure you don't destroy that Gospel unity because of your selfishness. We must not be complacent. Many a good church has been ruined by complacency. Christians are to live a life together that is worthy of the calling they have received. They are united through the Gospel, and so they are to preserve it at all costs in the Truth.

The Church's Diversity (vv. 7–12)

Whilst a church is unified, Christians are not uniform! Verse 7: 'But to each one of us grace has been given as Christ apportioned it.' Paul's point here is that the risen and ascended Christ has given each one of us unique gifts. We are uniquely made. Those gifts are given – our skills and talents are God-given, not to be used selfishly but for the benefit of others. The exalted Lord Jesus has given each one of us wonderful gifts to use. That is what Paul is saying in these slightly baffling words in verses 8–10. This is why it says:

> 'When he ascended on high,
> he led captives in his train
> and gave gifts to men.'

> (What does 'he ascended' mean except that he also descended to the lower, earthly regions? He who descended is the very one who ascended higher than all the heavens, in order to fill the whole universe.)

If you're confused about this passage then take comfort, you are not the first! Paul is quoting from Psalm 68 which tells how God goes up to his city, Zion, in victory leading a whole train of captives. He is giving out the booty of the victory. Paul sees that Jesus has fulfilled these verses by his own ascension and exaltation. The Jesus who came to earth, descended from heaven and who humbled himself, even to death on a cross, is the very same Jesus who now rules the heavens and equips his church. It is this risen and glorified Jesus who has given us gifts. In the New Testament there are about twenty such gifts mentioned but it is clear that those lists are not meant to be exhaustive. God's people have a whole range of gifts.

But in verse 11, Paul mentions four in particular. 'It was Jesus who gave some to be apostles, some to be prophets, some to be evangelists and some to be pastors and teachers.' Why does Paul single out these gifts? His reason is that these people have a unique role in preparing God's people for works of service. It is likely that Paul intends us to see the apostles and prophets as foundation gifts for the church. He says as much in 3:5 and 2:20. These are the original apostles and prophets of the Old Testament and New Testament who laid the foundation of the church and we have their teaching in the Bible. In this unique sense they have been and gone. But the evangelists and pastor-teachers (Paul links the words in the original) are still very much around and needed. The evangelists are, if you like, the spiritual midwives. They are the ones who lead others to new birth, who bring non-Christians to a faith in Christ. The pastor-teachers are those who teach the people of God. They have a job of shepherding the flock. That's what the word means. And they do it by teaching God's Word, by teaching the apostolic and prophetic foundations. As John Stott comments: 'Nothing builds up the church of God better than the Word of God.' So the reason that Paul mentions these gifts in particular is because these are essential for the growth of the body. As Paul says, they prepare God's people for works of service. Without evangelists and pastor-teachers, the church will die. That's why good and godly leadership is so essential for the body, and it is why there are more stringent tests for leaders in the New Testament than anyone else. They will be held accountable for their work. That is why we do so need to pray for those who teach God's Word. It is a serious business, and they need our prayers as they do that work.

But what does that mean for the rest of the body? Paul says that they are prepared for works of service. The idea is *every member* ministry. The church is not meant to be a bus: the pastor at the driver's seat, maybe the curate taking the fares, but everyone else sitting on the bus enjoying the ride. No, the church is like an orchestra, everyone playing their part, with the leader keeping everyone in time. Everyone is special. Many Christians down the ages have exalted the vicar or pastor above their station. Someone visiting America from Britain had seen three types of toilet: 'Men, women, clergy.' This only reinforces the stereotypes. Yes, the pastor is important but he's not that important. He is simply one of the body, where everyone has a role to play. We are diverse, uniquely gifted by the risen and exalted Lord Jesus to do works of service.

Every Christian therefore needs to ask of their relationship to a church: Are we just along for the ride? Or are we using our God-given gifts for the benefit of the whole body? For every person, there is another gift. That is the joy of being part of a body. No one has everything. Everyone has something. For some it will mean getting stuck in where previously you haven't. Maybe others will be thinking, 'I feel I can offer less than I used to be able.' But it is important to realise that just by turning up on a Sunday you are encouraging others. It all counts. It's like the conductor who stopped the orchestra one day and said: 'I can't hear the triangle!' Every part matters, and when one bit is not functioning the whole body is affected. Each of God's people is to do works of service for the benefit of the body. Are you involved? Or are you just a spectator? A church is united in its diversity.

The Church's Maturity (vv. 12–16)

This is the goal of a church: maturity. In verse 13: Paul says that these gifted evangelists and teachers are there to prepare God's people for works of service so that the body of Christ may be built up 'until we all reach unity in the faith and in the knowledge of the Son of God and become mature, attaining to the whole measure of the fullness of Christ.' There is a sense, of course, in which this will not happen completely until we get to heaven. Only there will we have complete unity and maturity, and only there will we attain to the measure of the fullness of Christ, that is be like Jesus perfectly. And yet our task in this life is to press on as far down that road as we can together in God's strength. We will be longing to grow in understanding and love of Christ together. We will be longing to be more united in our focus and mission.

It is vital to recognise that Paul understands this maturity to be corporate. As individuals we will be growing each day in Christ-likeness, and yet we need one another to do that. One day we'll be presented before God as a mature, fully formed body, with Christ as our head. He says literally that we will become a 'complete person'. We cannot be maturing in our own Christian lives unless we are also contributing to our fellow brothers' and sisters' maturity. If you have a rather relaxed view of church, a take it or leave it attitude, then Paul would want to question your maturity. He would say you're still a babe!

It is worth asking the question: Am I growing in the faith, that is, growing more mature in the knowledge of Jesus Christ? For only then can you resist the winds and waves of doctrine. So many young Christians are blown about by the latest fads and theological crazes. If we are to steer a good course, then we need the rudder of God's Word and the support of one another to do it.

There was a story reported of how a group of English tourists managed to be rescued from the seas off Bali in the Indonesian archipelago. They were rescued because one of the girls on board their stricken ship sent a text message on her mobile phone to her boyfriend in Cornwall, and so the Cornish Coastguard managed to contact the Indonesian authorities, via Australia's coastguard. And yet for over twenty-four hours, these young men and women were at the mercy of the high waves and ocean currents because they had no engine and their rudder wouldn't work. But the healthy Christian church need not be tossed around in this stormy world if it is anchored in God's Word and is seeking to apply it to its lifestyle. That is what Paul means when he tells the Ephesians that they need to be speaking the truth in love. He's not simply talking about not lying. Literally the word means '"truthing" in love'. They are lovingly to apply the truth to their lives and to help one another to do so. Then they will be a growing and maturing church, growing up into Christ their head, as each part of the body fulfils its role. That's how a church matures: when the Word of God is taught and applied and lived out in love together with other Christians. It's a wonderful picture isn't it? A fully working, maturing, growing and loving body. That's our maturity.

Which would you prefer? To be a 'castaway' Christian or to be part of this great body that Paul is teaching here? At the end of the day, there is no such thing as a castaway Christian. It is a contradiction in terms. All of us act like it sometimes. All of us should repent of it. Rather, Paul teaches that we are a living, breathing and growing body: a body that is united around the Gospel and living in love; a body that has many diverse gifts with each part contributing to the growth; and a body which is maturing, fed on the Word of God and growing more like Jesus.

6

The Model Church
1 Thessalonians 1

Paul, Silas and Timothy,

To the church of the Thessalonians in God the Father and the Lord Jesus Christ:

Grace and peace to you.

We always thank God for all of you, mentioning you in our prayers. We continually remember before our God and Father your work produced by faith, your labor prompted by love, and your endurance inspired by hope in our Lord Jesus Christ.

For we know, brothers loved by God, that he has chosen you, because our gospel came to you not simply with words, but also with power, with the Holy Spirit and with deep conviction. You know how we lived among you for your sake. You became imitators of us and of the Lord; in spite of severe suffering, you welcomed the message with the joy given by the Holy Spirit. And so you became a model to all the believers in Macedonia and Achaia. The Lord's message rang out from you not only in Macedonia and Achaia – your faith in God has

become known everywhere. Therefore we do not need to say
anything about it, for they themselves report what kind of
reception you gave us. They tell how you turned to God from
idols to serve the living and true God, and to wait for his Son
from heaven, whom he raised from the dead – Jesus, who res-
cues us from the coming wrath.

'Pastor, what can we do about our son?' In a flood of
tears the story came out. This was a couple who had
worked and prayed hard to raise their children in the
Christian faith. They loved God and so naturally they
wanted their children to love him too. But their eldest
son, who had just gone to college, decided to throw in
everything he had been taught from childhood. He told
his parents quite bluntly that he didn't want anything to
do with God anymore.

You don't have to be in the ministry all that long
before you come across a story like that. Why do so
many young people abandon the faith of their youth? A
few years ago a team of sociologists in America decided
to find out by polling hundreds of university students.
They published their findings in the *Review of Religious
Research*. They discovered that the number one reason
given for abandoning the Christian faith was hypocrisy
at 38 per cent. They were put off by the behaviour of
church members, which contradicted their professed
beliefs.

However, it also has to be said that while many are
switched off Christianity because of the behaviour of professing Christians, many are turned on because of what
they see in Christian lives. Here are some words of a
physics student:

When I started as a student, you were likely to find me
on the footy pitch or in a pub on a Sunday, certainly not

in church. While I didn't have a religious upbringing, I
did on occasions wonder what it was all about. . . .
Coming to college was the first time I met committed
Christians of my own age. To my surprise they were
intelligent people who didn't seem particularly gullible.
So I was intrigued. . . . One thing that struck me was the
integrity of lifestyle displayed by Christians. They had
better, more real friendships and better attitudes to other
people. This is a generalization, but I didn't find the
hypocrisy that the media are so keen to expose in
the established church.

It is all to do with modelling. There are those who badly
model the Christian faith with the result that people turn
away because of hypocrisy, and by way of contrast there
are those who model so well what it means to be a
Christian that the result is that even some of
Christianity's most vociferous critics are often reduced
to silent admiration.

But it is not simply individual Christians who need to
model the new life which is to be found in Jesus Christ;
whole Christian communities need to do it too. This is
the way the American writer Richard Neuhaus lays
down the challenge: 'The church best serves the world
when it is most distinctively and unapologetically the
church. . . . When the church dares to be different, it
models for the world what God calls the world to
become. The church models what it means to be a community of caring and a community of character.' Just
what it means to be a model church is discovered by
turning to the first letter of the Thessalonians.

We discover that this was a *mimicking church*. 'You
became imitators of us and of the Lord' (v. 6). They
looked to Paul and Silas as model Christians and copied
them as Paul and Silas copied Jesus. As a result they in

turn became a *model church* for others to emulate: 'And so *you* became a model to *all* the believers in Macedonia and Achaia' (v. 7). That is one great compliment being paid, for other Christians living miles away to say, 'We want to be like them. That is exactly how our church ought to be.'

When the word 'church' is mentioned what is the picture which springs to most people's mind? A building, perhaps with gothic architecture, cold and unprepossessing. Maybe an institution like 'the Church of England'. Or it could be a career move; we talk of people going 'into the church'. None of these common ideas is found here. Verse 1 literally reads: 'To a church of Thessalonians.' It is like writing a letter addressed to a 'church' of Yorkshiremen. There is nothing particularly religious about the word 'church' (*ekklesia*). It is simply a way of saying 'a group of Thessalonians'. How this group was pulled together is described in Acts 17:10. There we are told that the apostle Paul and a few friends turned up in town and made a bee-line to the synagogue following their usual strategy of targetting the Jews first. Arguing from the Scriptures they tried to persuade them that Jesus was God's appointed and long awaited King who had to suffer and rise from the dead. Luke informs us that *some were persuaded (v. 4)*. This was not just an emotional experience; they became convinced of the truth. In addition to some Jews, a good number of Greeks, as well as a number of well-to-do women, also became followers of this Christ. But then some of the synagogue Jews became hostile and with 'rent-a-mob' ran Paul and his friends out of town. We are therefore talking about a time period of no more than three to four weeks to gather a group of believers by preaching the Gospel, carry out some follow-up talks on Christian basics, and that was it: the model church was formed!

We don't know how many there were, but the chances are that it was no more than fifty or sixty people. Nonetheless this gathering had become the model for the entire region.

We might therefore want to ask: what is so special about this group of Christians with very little by way of organisational structure – no special building, no organ, no 'full time' minister, but which nonetheless propels Paul into rapturous praise of God? There are four features of this model church that are particularly striking and which modern-day churches need to emulate.

A Supernatural Community

First of all, this was no ordinary gathering, it was supernatural. This is evident in the full description Paul gives of them in verse 1: 'To the group of Thessalonians *in* God the Father and the Lord Jesus Christ, grace and peace to you.' This means that by virtue of these people accepting Paul's message that Jesus is the Lord of the universe, they are drawn into the very presence of the God they never knew. They now inhabit a divine environment. As these people are gathered together by the Word of God, the Gospel, they are taken into the very heart of God, bathed in his glory, infused with his energy, hedged in by his love. They are 'in' God and the Lord Jesus. They have discovered a most wonderful thing; they have found that God's nature is grace and peace. It is not so much that God *gives* grace, rather that he is gracious; that is the type of God he is: he is a kind God who loves to give and keep on giving. This is the God who stoops down to lift us up like a Father would lift up his little child. What is more this is the God who makes peace, having taken all the steps necessary to remove the enmity between himself

and us caused by our snubbing him and wounding him,
by being wounded for us on a cross. Accordingly, this
God will never be against us. He will never condemn us.
Peace has broken out with the result that heaven meets
earth when God's people meet in his name. When these
Christians gathered in Thessalonica they were coming
into the presence of divine royalty. This is also the case
whenever Christians meet today, however humble their
surroundings and low their number.

A Persuaded Community

These people were also convinced by truth: 'We always
thank God for all of you, mentioning you in our
prayers. We continually remember before our God and
Father your work produced by faith, your labor
prompted by love, and your endurance inspired by
hope in our Lord Jesus Christ.' As we have seen in Acts
17, when these people became Christians, they are not
described as being converted, but as having been *persuaded*. That is, their minds were engaged as they
listened very carefully to Paul's arguments about who
Jesus is and what he has done. So New Testament evangelism always involves the mind. But it doesn't stop at
the mind; it filters down to capture the whole person
leading to a totally different way of thinking and behav-
ing; a complete reordering of values and just what it is
we are to live for. What we have here is the three-fold
experience of all of those who have become convinced
of the divine humanity, sacrificial death and glorious
resurrection of Jesus: they have faith, love and hope.
Faith, directed upwards towards God; love, directed
outwards towards others; hope, reaching onwards into
the future to Jesus.

If Jesus died for me and is alive, then I am invited to trust him. Can we honestly think that the God of the universe would go to such lengths to bring us into a personal relationship with himself and then make a mistake and lose us somewhere along the way? Of course not. When he was on earth no one who put their trust in him was ever disappointed. Whether it was a leper cut off from society, a prostitute spurned by the religious establishment, or a broken-hearted widow who had just lost her only son. They could all come to Jesus and he was there for them. We can have faith.

But if Jesus is the King who was broken on a cross, with my sin holding him there, then I have been loved beyond all human comprehension. Jesus cannot love me any more or any less than he did when he first loved me and died for me. The love that led him from heaven to occupy a cold, dark grave is the same love that he pours out on me today. Consequently, I will love him and be enabled by him to love others too. We can know love.

Also if Jesus is the Christ risen from the dead who has promised to return in glory, then Christians, of all people, can be positive about the future. What a future that is going to be, when the One who is goodness and beauty and holiness shall reign; a future in which everything is caught up into his life-giving personality. We can have hope.

What is more, all of these things have an observable effect in the here and now. Paul talks about their *work* produced by faith, their *labour* prompted by love and their *endurance* inspired by hope. What is work? It is energy expended. What is labour? It is persevering when the going gets tough. What is endurance? It is continuing to work in spite of the tiredness.

We might well ask: what is our picture of how the Christian life should be? What does a properly functioning church look like? Let us try a sketch. It is a people so trusting in Jesus that they are willing to work hard for him. It is a people so full of love that they get tired out for him. It is a people so full of hope that they put up with all sorts of unpleasantness and inconvenience for him. So what sort of Christians are we? Is this our experience? Working so hard for him that at times we are just plain tired out, but going on anyway because we love him? Do we try and cope with those upsets and work at relationships with other Christians, as well as putting ourselves out for non-Christians, knowing that one day Jesus is going to return and that this life is so short anyway that we want to make the most of it for him? According to Paul's teaching here, that is what we should expect; it is a sure sign that God is at work.

A Chosen Community

How did this happen? Is it because these folk were smarter than others in Thessalonica? Is it because they had been let in to some inside spiritual track denied to others? Not at all: 'For we know, brothers loved by God, that he has chosen you.' Paul is not congratulating these people for their faith, he is thanking God for it, because he is the one who gives it. He has *chosen* them. We sometimes talk of us making a decision for Christ. True. But here Paul speaks of Christ making a decision for us, which is much more remarkable.

How can Paul be so sure that we have been chosen by the kindness of God to know him and be loved by him? That is a very important question. Paul tells us, which is the meaning of that little word 'because' in v. 5a: 'because our gospel came to you not simply with words, but also with power, with the Holy Spirit and with deep conviction.'

A Transformed Community

These people have been changed almost beyond recognition, which is the focus of the rest of the passage. And this transformation has been effected by 'a Word', the word of the Gospel. They *received the word* (vv. 5–6); they *proclaimed the word* (vv. 7–8); and they *lived the word* (v. 9).

These people became Christians, forming a new community of transformed people, because first of all they received a message: 'Because our gospel came to you not simply with words, but also with power, with the Holy Spirit and with deep conviction. You know how we lived among you for your sake. You became imitators of us and of the Lord; in spite of severe suffering, you welcomed the message with the joy given by the Holy Spirit.' As Paul explained the Gospel, that message came to them as more than mere human words. It came with power, provided by God himself, the Holy Spirit, with the result that those who heard it were convinced that as Paul spoke, God was speaking through him. Paul is not saying that *alongside* his message some other thing happened that showed the Holy Spirit's power. Rather, when the message was preached and disciples were produced, God's power was at work. According to Genesis 1, God spoke his Word, which went out with his Spirit just like our words are carried along on our breath, and the universe was brought into being. Likewise, the new miracle is that as the message of the Gospel is explained that too goes out with God's Spirit to bring about a new creation: a church.

What is it that we think will bring our non-Christian friends to faith in Jesus? A miracle or two or some enthusiastic singing perhaps? According to the apostle it will be the Christian message faithfully taught, applied by the Holy Spirit. Changed lives are also part of that witness. That is why Paul says 'you know how we behaved amongst you'. It is no good saying one thing and doing something else which contradicts it – that leads to the falling away with which we began. Christian behaviour must back up Christian belief.

What is more, Christians will invariably proclaim the message too. 'And so you became a model to all the believers in Macedonia and Achaia. The Lord's message rang out from you not only in Macedonia and Achaia – your faith in God has become known everywhere. Therefore we do not need to say anything about it' (vv. 7–8). Have you ever wondered why we do not find any exhortation in the New Testament letters to evangelise? It is because it would have been like writing a letter to someone encouraging them to breathe. It just happened naturally. Just as when someone pulls a rope with a bell attached to the end of it, it rings, so those who know the Lord Jesus will in a variety of ways be spreading the Gospel.

All of these things are summed up in verse 9. As they lived the word, in down-to-earth, observable ways, there was a total change in direction: 'For they themselves report what kind of reception you gave us. They tell how you turned to God from idols to serve the living and true God, and to wait for his Son from heaven, whom he raised from the dead – Jesus, who rescues us from the coming wrath.' First, we are to notice that they welcomed God's messengers. We would do well to remember the words of Jesus speaking to his disciples: 'He who receives you receives me, and he who receives me receives the One who sent me' (Mt. 10:40).

The second thing we are to take note of is that they turn from idols, that is, anything which occupies the place of God in our lives: what we live for, eat, breath and sleep for. It might be a sport, it might be a career or it might be another person, but more often than not it is ourselves. But now it is to be Jesus.

Which leads to the third feature, turning to 'serve the living and true God [that is, God as he really is and not how we like to imagine him to be] and to wait for his Son from heaven, whom he raised from the dead – Jesus who rescues us from the coming wrath.' What is all that but faith, love and hope? Trusting in God and not idols: faith; serving him: love; and waiting for Jesus: hope.

What has Jesus come to rescue us from? Adolescent boredom? Mid-life stress? No, but from the wrath to come. That is when we shall really see what it means to be saved, just as a person knows what it is to be rescued as they are pulled from a burning building. Then words will not be able to express the immense gratitude we shall feel to this wonderful God who knowingly and willingly went to the cross to spare us that pain. Surely, this is a God who deserves our trust, who calls forth our love and inspires our hope. This is the God of the model church.

7

The Care of the Church
Acts 20:17–38

From Miletus, Paul sent to Ephesus for the elders of the church. When they arrived, he said to them: 'You know how I lived the whole time I was with you, from the first day I came into the province of Asia. I served the Lord with great humility and with tears, although I was severely tested by the plots of the Jews. You know that I have not hesitated to preach anything that would be helpful to you but have taught you publicly and from house to house. I have declared to both Jews and Greeks that they must turn to God in repentance and have faith in our Lord Jesus.

And now, compelled by the Spirit, I am going to Jerusalem, not knowing what will happen to me there. I only know that in every city the Holy Spirit warns me that prison and hardships are facing me. However, I consider my life worth nothing to me, if only I may finish the race and complete the task the Lord Jesus has given me – the task of testifying to the gospel of God's grace.

Now I know that none of you among whom I have gone about preaching the kingdom will ever see me again. Therefore, I declare to you today that I am innocent of the blood of all men. For I have not hesitated to proclaim to you the whole will of God. Keep watch over yourselves and all the flock of which the Holy Spirit has made you overseers. Be shepherds of the church of God, which he bought with his own blood. I know that after I leave, savage wolves will come in among you and will not spare the flock. Even from your own number men will arise and distort the truth in order to draw away disciples after them. So be on your guard! Remember that for three years I never stopped warning each of you night and day with tears.

Now I commit you to God and to the word of his grace, which can build you up and give you an inheritance among all those who are sanctified. I have not coveted anyone's silver or gold or clothing. You yourselves know that these hands of mine have supplied my own needs and the needs of my companions. In everything I did, I showed you that by this kind of hard work we must help the weak, remembering the words the Lord Jesus himself said: 'It is more blessed to give than to receive.'

When he had said this, he knelt down with all of them and prayed. They all wept as they embraced him and kissed him. What grieved them most was his statement that they would never see his face again. Then they accompanied him to the ship.

What is your picture of the successful Christian minister? Here is one author writing with his tongue firmly placed in his cheek:

The modern pastor is expected to be a preacher, counsellor, administrator, PR guru, fundraiser and hand-holder. Depending upon the size of the church he serves, he may have to be an expert on youth, something of an accountant, janitor, evangelist, small groups expert, an excellent chair of committees, a team-player and a transparent leader. Of course his home life must be exemplary and he should never appear tired or discouraged, since he must always be spiritual, prayerful, warm-hearted, and passionate but unflappable. He should spend no fewer than 40 hours a week in sermon preparation, no fewer than 30 hours in counselling, at least 20 hours in regular visitation of his flock, and another 15 hours in door-to-door evangelism, and at least 20 hours on administration, another 10 on hospital calling, leaving about 50 hours for miscellaneous matters (especially being available if anyone wants to see him day or night). And then a neighbour will ask his wife: 'Excuse me, I don't mean to be rude, but I'd really like to know "What does your husband do the rest of his time, apart from, you know, his work on Sundays?"'

As we have seen, in Ephesians 4 it is quite clear that the whole of God's people are to be involved in works of service, that is, in ministry. But what is the specific role of the ordained minister, the pastor-teacher? How is that minister to equip and encourage the different members of the church to develop and use their God-given gifts? Obviously not by being the all-knowing, all-competent do-it-all! In fact one could not have a better job description of the pastor-teacher than the one presented in Acts 20.

The Model of Caring

The model for caring for a church is provided by the apostle Paul himself. The fact that in the midst of a very busy schedule Paul took time out to meet with these church leaders at all is in itself a testimony to Paul's dedicated pastoral care. As we read in verse 16, Paul was in a desperate hurry to get to Jerusalem by Pentecost. Time was of a premium. But like any good leader of God's people, Paul is never too busy to make time to meet people's needs. Certainly, he couldn't go to the church in Ephesus itself, so he does something much more effective strategically, he calls together those who on a day-to-day basis work within the church.

These leaders are referred to as *elders* in verse 17, overseers or 'bishops' whose function is pasturing in verse 28a (literally *shepherding*, v. 28b). All the terms refer to the same office. The actual title is not as important as what the leaders are meant to be doing; it is how oversight or 'bishoping' takes place that is of supreme significance.

In this emotionally charged atmosphere Paul reminds them how he has worked non-stop in Ephesus for three solid years. First, he draws attention to *his way of life*, 'You know how I lived the *whole time* I was with you from the first day I came to the Province of Asia' (vv. 18–19). In other words, he was totally consistent from the beginning of his ministry to the end. He planted the church, he nurtured it and protected it. This was no fly-by-night evangelist who had ulterior motives which were financially driven. On the contrary, as we see in verse 33–5, Paul was so concerned not to be a burden or even appear to be 'on the make' that he did some moonlighting to support himself and then gave money away so that he might fulfil Jesus' saying, 'It is more blessed to give than to receive.' He gave of his time, talents and money.

Neither was it a matter of impressive showmanship, the omnicompetent minister exuding confidence and charisma. Far from it, 'I served [literally slaved for] the Lord with great humility and with tears, although I was severely tested by the plots of the Jews' (v. 19). In other words, although he may well have been tempted to take short cuts in his work and get out of an uncomfortable situation made almost unbearable because of the pressures contrived by the Jews to get rid of him, nonetheless he remained. This may well account for the tears of which Paul speaks; it was simply breaking his heart – his own people had turned against him – however, he saw it as his duty and privilege to be 'serving the Lord'.

That is the real test of authentic Gospel ministry, to go on when the pressure to give up is so great.

One of the most influential clergymen of the early part of the nineteenth century was Charles Simeon of Cambridge. He was an extraordinary preacher of the Gospel. When he arrived as Vicar of Holy Trinity Church, the normal congregation, who didn't want him, simply didn't turn up. The church wardens locked all the pews so those who did attend couldn't sit down. Eventually some started to come along and were converted. They had to stand in the aisles throughout the service and even then Simeon was only allowed to have one service in the morning. At his own expense he brought some chairs and set up benches for people to sit on. These the wardens threw out into the churchyard. This went on for five years. His ministry lasted for 50 years. When he began he couldn't find a single person who would even say 'good morning' to him. At his funeral the whole town turned out to pay tribute to a great and godly man. Gospel ministry involves tears and toil; there is no escape as there was no escape for Paul.

The Method of Caring

How, then, did Paul go about caring for the people of God, shepherding the sheep? 'You know that I did not [literally] shrink back from proclaiming anything that would be helpful to you but taught you publicly and from house to house' (v. 20).

Let us think about this imagery of the shepherd for a moment. One of the primary duties of a shepherd is to feed the sheep, or, to be more precise, to lead the sheep to the place where they can graze on good pasture. So it is with God's spiritual shepherds. Their task is not to entertain the flock but to feed the sheep from the nourishing pasture of God's Word. Therefore, as we have seen on several occasions in our study, first and foremost pastoral ministry is a teaching ministry. This is brought out by the verbs used by Paul to describe what he has been doing during his three years in Ephesus: he has 'preached' (v. 20), 'taught' (v. 20), 'declared' (v. 21), 'testified' (v. 24), 'preached' (v. 25), 'proclaimed' (v. 27) and 'warned' (v. 31).

The true Christian minister who really does care for the sheep has two aims in mind. First, to lead to faith in Christ those who have no faith. As Paul puts it in verse 21, 'I have declared to both Jews and Greeks that they must turn to God in repentance and have faith in the Lord Jesus Christ.' While a minister may not particularly have the *gift* of an evangelist (we can't all be Billy Grahams!), he must do the *work* of an evangelist, as Paul says elsewhere to his assistant Timothy (2 Tim. 4:5).

Second, the minister is to build up the faith in Christ of those who do have faith: 'I did not shrink back from proclaiming to you the whole will of God' (v. 27); 'I commit you to God and to the *word* of his grace which can *build you* up' (v. 32). Paul wasn't selective about what he taught and to whom he taught it. He didn't hold back because some things were difficult or unpopular: questions of heaven and hell; divine sovereignty and human responsibility; sexual ethics; the exclusivity of Jesus as being the only way of salvation; and so on. Paul was of the view that if God had revealed it, he had a duty to teach it.

This does not mean that the minister is free from the temptation to cut and tailor his message to please his congregation. We all like to be liked, if not then there is something pathological about us! Therefore, the pressure will constantly be present to compromise when, for example, the minister seeks to speak from a passage of Scripture which goes against the current trends of society.

A few years ago a well-known Bible teacher from Britain was speaking at a minister's conference in New Zealand. This is a country where radical feminism is rampant both in the church and society in general, where in some quarters it is almost compulsory to refer to God as 'Mother' and the Holy Spirit as 'our sister'. The group was examining what the Bible taught about the differing roles and responsibilities between men and women. They were agreed as to the clarity of Scripture on some of these points. But one of the ministers stood up and, speaking for many of his colleagues, said, 'Yes, but if I were to teach that in my church I would be crucified.' These fears are very real and a constant source of vexation for those who wish to be faithful to the Scriptures.

With Paul ministers must proclaim the *whole will of God to the whole people of God*. That is why there is tremendous value in expository preaching, that is, to work through a book or a passage and let the Bible speak for itself. It is good practice to try to parcel it out over the course of a year so one covers Old Testament, Gospels, Letters, major doctrines and matters of Christian living that we face today. That way, it is the Word and not the World which sets the agenda. The world raises certain questions, like 'Why is there suffering?' But God too wants to raise with us his questions: 'Why are you so rebellious? Why don't you recognise the utter folly of living without me? Come to know the truth in my Son and then you will be free.' Certainly the Word must engage with the world (expository preaching is not dull verse-by-verse commentary), but it is that Word that is given priority over and against, for example, the preacher's pet subjects. With Paul, the 'whole counsel of God' is to be taught.

By way of extending this principle one might ask: How much are those who are Christian husbands and fathers in our congregations encouraging their own families to understand and apply the Word of God? When the family watches the TV together or has a meal together, why not say, 'Let's just think about what we have heard or watched from a Christian point of view.' How proactive are parents or grandparents in getting God's truth into their children's and grandchildren's lives? There is so much value in buying that book which will help or that tape with a good message, as well as encouraging them along to Sunday school and showing by one's own example that we take the Gospel seriously. Do they ever catch *us* reading a Bible or a Christian book? It was 'publically and from *house to house*' that Paul made it his aim to teach the whole will of God, and surely the aim of every Christian should not be any less.

If the minister is to feed the sheep with the Word, he is also to protect the sheep with that same Word. There are crooks as well as shepherds. In verses 25–9 Paul foresees dangers from without – 'After I leave savage wolves will come in' (v. 29); he also speaks of dangers from within – 'Even from your *own* number men will arise' (v. 30). The church is an endangered species. There is never a moment when it is not under threat. Just as it is built up by the truth of God, it is torn down by the lies and half-truths of Satan. Wolves have only one aim, to harm the sheep. They may well be sincere – wolves are consistently wolf-like, true to their natures – but they are dangerous.

Prior to the 1998 Lambeth conference, the worldwide gathering of Anglican Bishops, Bishop John Spong of Newark, New Jersey, issued 12 theses for a new reformation. These included the view that 'theism' as a way of defining God was dead and that the concept of Jesus as a kind of incarnation of God was 'nonsensical'. He also rejected the idea of Jesus dying for our sins, the authority of Scripture and the existence of universally binding moral principles. Not surprisingly during the 24 years during which he was Bishop church membership in his diocese fell by 35 per cent, 81 per cent faster than the national rate of decline.

Perhaps what is more disturbing is the fact that some from *within* this good apostolically founded church would spring up and through a distortion of the truth draw people away after them, which means away from the teaching of the apostles. Not that they necessarily set out to do that, wanting to form another church (though some will). Often it happens through a gradual drift, by not keeping a check on their own spiritual lives. That is why this prophecy is prefaced in verse 28 with a warning to the leaders: 'Keep watch over *yourselves* and the flock.' The sobering reality is that there is no reason in principle why any 'sound' evangelical minister could not one day find themselves distorting God's truth; history is littered with examples. That is why pastors need pastoring too – by the congregation. This will involve their prayers, offering feedback, encouragement as well as being constructively critical. It is also why ministers need to go to conferences where they can be fed and kept on course. Many of us have all seen those old black

and white hammy werewolf films. The moon comes out
and the poor fellow starts to grow excessive hair on his
hands and then his face. It is a *gradual* transformation. So
is the spiritual degeneration that can occur, whereby
gamekeeper is changed into poacher.

This is what the great Puritan minister, Richard
Baxter, says in his unpacking of this passage in his book
The Reformed Pastor:

> It is possible for preaching to succeed in the salvation of
> others without bringing holiness to our own hearts or
> lives. Many shall say on that day, 'Lord, have we not
> prophesied in your name?' and they will be answered: 'I
> never knew you; depart from me you who work iniquity'
> (Mt. 7:23). How many have preached Christ and yet per-
> ished because they lacked a saving interest in Christ?

That is how vulnerable ministers are, and there are times
they feel it intensely.

The Motivation for Caring

What could possibly keep a person going through all the
hard work, temptations and disappointments that
attend Word ministry in the pulpit, in the homegroups,
in the Sunday schools? In verse 28 Paul tells us: 'Keep
watch over yourselves and all the flock of which the
Holy Spirit has made you overseers. Be shepherds of the
church of God which he bought with *His own blood*.' No
church is the minister's church in terms of its being his
possession. It is *God's* church. All three persons of the
Trinity have invested themselves in gathering this flock
together. It is God the Father who decided to save us. It
is God the Son who bled for us. It is God the Holy Spirit

who lives in us and gives us ministers to take care of us. To know that he was caring for the precious children of God was all the motivation Paul needed to have in order to keep on keeping on. So much so that his main concern was not losing his life but ending his life well: 'And now compelled by the Spirit, I am going to Jerusalem, not knowing what will happen to me there [here is an apostle who didn't know the future; so why should we?]. I only know that in every city the Holy Spirit warns me that prison and hardships await me. *However*, I consider my life worth nothing to me, if only I may *finish* the race and *complete* the task the Lord Jesus has given me – the task of testifying to the gospel of God's grace' (vv. 22–4). To start the ministry is a fairly easy thing to do: one is usually young and full of idealism. The challenge is finishing the ministry as one began it. That will only happen if we encourage each other to see the church as Christ sees it: infinitely precious, worthy of our care and utmost attention. As we would hopefully go out of our way to care for our own family, we are to go to any lengths to care for God's family in God's way, gently ministering the unchanging Word of Truth.

8

Worship in the Church
Hebrews 12:18 – 13:21

You have not come to a mountain that can be touched and that is burning with fire; to darkness, gloom and storm; to a trumpet blast or to such a voice speaking words that those who heard it begged that no further word be spoken to them, because they could not bear what was commanded: 'If even an animal touches the mountain, it must be stoned.' The sight was so terrifying that Moses said, 'I am trembling with fear.'

But you have come to Mount Zion, to the heavenly Jerusalem, the city of the living God. You have come to thousands upon thousands of angels in joyful assembly, to the church of the firstborn, whose names are written in heaven. You have come to God, the judge of all men, to the spirits of righteous men made perfect, to Jesus the mediator of a new covenant, and to the sprinkled blood that speaks a better word than the blood of Abel.

See to it that you do not refuse him who speaks. If they did not escape when they refused him who warned them on earth, how much less will we, if we turn away from him who warns us from heaven? At that time his voice shook the earth, but now he has promised, 'Once more I will shake not only the earth but also the heavens.' The words 'once more' indicate the removing of what can be shaken-that is, created things-so that what cannot be shaken may remain.

Therefore, since we are receiving a kingdom that cannot be shaken, let us be thankful, and so worship God acceptably with reverence and awe, for our 'God is a consuming fire.' Keep on loving each other as brothers. Do not forget to entertain strangers, for by so doing some people have entertained angels without knowing it. Remember those in prison as if you were their fellow prisoners, and those who are mistreated as if you yourselves were suffering.

Marriage should be honored by all, and the marriage bed kept pure, for God will judge the adulterer and all the sexually immoral. Keep your lives free from the love of money and be content with what you have, because God has said,

'Never will I leave you;
never will I forsake you.'
So we say with confidence,

'The Lord is my helper; I will not be afraid.
What can man do to me?'

Remember your leaders, who spoke the word of God to you. Consider the outcome of their way of life and imitate their faith. Jesus Christ is the same yesterday and today and forever.

Do not be carried away by all kinds of strange teachings. It is good for our hearts to be strengthened by grace, not by ceremonial foods, which are of no value to those who eat them. We have an altar from which those who minister at the tabernacle have no right to eat.

The high priest carries the blood of animals into the Most Holy Place as a sin offering, but the bodies are burned outside the camp. And so Jesus also suffered outside the city gate to *make the people holy through his own blood. Let us, then, go to him outside the camp, bearing the disgrace he bore. For here we do not have an enduring city, but we are looking for the city that is to come.*

Through Jesus, therefore, let us continually offer to God a sacrifice of praise-the fruit of lips that confess his name. And do not forget to do good and to share with others, for with such sacrifices God is pleased.

Obey your leaders and submit to their authority. They keep watch over you as men who must give an account. Obey them so that their work will be a joy, not a burden, for that would be of no advantage to you.

Pray for us. We are sure that we have a clear conscience and desire to live honorably in every way. I particularly urge you to pray so that I may be restored to you soon.

May the God of peace, who through the blood of the eternal covenant brought back from the dead our Lord Jesus, that great Shepherd of the sheep, equip you with everything good for doing his will, and may he work in us what is pleasing to him, through Jesus Christ, to whom be glory for ever and ever. Amen.

Are you a BC Christian or an AD Christian?

You may say that the answer is obvious, since we live *after* Christ we must all be *Anno Domini* 'in the Year of our Lord' Christians; what else could we be? Chronologically that may well be true, but *theologically*, it is only too possible for people to be BC Christians to the extent that what they do when they meet together as church is more closely patterned on Old Testament practices than those of the New Testament. They act as if the coming of Jesus hardly makes any difference at all. And whether a church is functioning as a BC church or an AD church is shown by their view of what constitutes 'worship'.

Worship is 'In'

It would be true to say that during the last twenty-five years or so amongst those churches which would own the label 'evangelical', a significant change in understanding has taken place over the meaning of the word 'worship'. If a few decades ago the person leading the service had said, 'We are now going to have a time of worship', most people would have looked on in utter bewilderment. Now everyone would know exactly what to expect: a lengthy time of contemporary Christian songs, maybe interspersed with a few prayers and exhortations, perhaps with hands held up in the air and a far-away look in the eyes.

What may come as a surprise is that nowhere in the New Testament is the word 'worship' ever used to describe what Christians did when they met together. It is never said that they met 'for worship'. This is particularly striking given that when the Jews met together in the temple or the Gentiles in their pagan shrines, it was precisely for 'worship' that they gathered. The absence of worship language to describe what Christians are meant to do as a church is evident in the writings of the apostle Paul. One scholar, Robert Banks, puts it like this: 'One of the most puzzling features of Paul's understanding of the church for his contemporaries, whether Jew or Gentile, must have been his failure to say that a person went to church primarily to 'worship'. Not once in his writings does he suggest that this is the case. . . .' Why? The answer is that something has happened of such epoch-making proportions that our view of worship can never be the same. What that something is has separated human history into two parts – BC and AD. That something is, of course, the birth, life, death and resurrection of Jesus Christ.

What's the Difference?

Let us take a look at worship BC and AD, noting the difference Jesus makes and the difficulties we get ourselves into if we forget that difference.

First of all, according to the Bible: what is worship? Someone who has looked at the biblical evidence in some detail and has come up with a definition that does justice to it is Dr David Peterson who defines worship in these terms: 'The worship of the living and true God is essentially an engagement with Him on the terms he proposes and in the way he alone makes possible.' By speaking of 'engaging with God', we are immediately drawn towards the idea that it is an activity that is much bigger than singing songs and saying prayers. For example, when someone engages, say, with their wife or husband, it is at all sorts of different levels. Certainly, it involves saying nice things, singing praises if you will; but it also involves working together, planning together, making friends and raising a family together, to name just a few of the joint activities which make up a couple's 'engaging'. In other words, it embraces the *whole* of life. And so it is with our engaging with God. At heart we are talking about a relationship. But this is a relationship which can only be conducted effectively on God's terms, not ours. What is more, he alone is the one who can open up the way so that the relationship – or worship – can happen in the first instance. Many people, as we shall see, tend to think of 'worship' as something *we* do for God, but first and foremost it arises out of something *he* alone does for us.

Gimme that Old Time Religion

The book in the Bible that gives us insight into worship BC, Old Testament style, in contrast to worship AD, Jesus style, is the letter to the Hebrews. When we turn to this letter and check out some of its references in the Old Testament we discover that the main idea of BC worship is *drawing near to God*.

Let us therefore briefly consider BC worship as we find it described in Hebrews 9:1–7:

> Now the first covenant had regulations for worship and also an earthly sanctuary. A tabernacle was set up. In its first room were the lampstand, the table and the consecrated bread; this was called the Holy Place. Behind the second curtain was a room called the Most Holy Place, which had the golden altar of incense and the gold-covered ark of the covenant. This ark contained the gold jar of manna, Aaron's staff that had budded, and the stone tablets of the covenant. Above the ark were the cherubim of the Glory, overshadowing the atonement cover. But we cannot discuss these things in detail now. When everything had been arranged like this, the priests entered regularly into the outer room to carry on their ministry. But only the high priest entered the inner room, and that only once a year, and never without blood, which he offered for himself and for the sins the people had committed in ignorance.

What is particularly characteristic about this description is that for people to worship what is needed is a holy man – a priest; who met in a holy place – a tent and later the temple; who did holy things – offer an animal sacrifice to turn away the anger of a holy God. The key idea is *'mediation'*. In fact, the temple in Jerusalem was designed to make a very clear statement, namely, 'keep your distance' which is something of a major setback if you wanted to draw near to God! The people who gathered at the temple encountered barrier after barrier. First

of all, there was the outer court, beyond which non-Jews
could not venture. Then there was an inner court,
beyond which women couldn't go. This was followed
by the court of Israel, beyond which men couldn't
progress. Finally, there was the priest's area leading to
the inner 'Holy of Holies', containing the ark of the
covenant – a golden box, symbolising God's presence –
hidden behind a thick screen. The high priest alone was
permitted to enter the Holy of Holies once a year to offer
a sacrifice for the sins of the people. In other words,
those who wanted to 'worship' God needed a go-
between, a mediator, to get through the barriers into
God's presence on their behalf. Such was the function of
the priest. It was one long complicated ritual of cleans-
ing and sacrifice, with the priests having to wear the
right type of clothes and carry out their little rituals in
the right way. However, an important lesson was being
taught by all of this; namely that it isn't an easy thing to
draw near to God. 'Worship' isn't simple. Why? Well,
because as we read in Hebrews 12:29 the true God is a
'consuming fire'. He is of such pure moral intensity that
if we were to approach him without some form of pro-
tective clothing, as it were, we would be burnt up. That
is what the religious system of Judaism provided; God's
appointed means of approaching him in safety.
Accordingly, in the Old Testament, worship was mainly,
but not exclusively, going to the right place, that is the
temple, and doing the right things: singing, praying,
dancing and sacrificing.

Now just imagine that with the coming of Jesus – the
God who became man – that the early Christians had
simply changed their *focus* of worship. Therefore,
instead of worshipping Jehovah, they worshipped Jesus
instead. What would have happened? The result would
have been a hybrid form of BC/AD worship, that is, Old

Testament worship modified. The early Christians would have built a special building in which to meet, whose architecture emphasised the remoteness of God, perhaps with an altar located at one end behind a screen. They would have had a special group of ministers called priests to perform special rituals, maybe offering some form of sacrifice to placate God. The only difference would have been that instead of singing praises and offering prayers in the name of Jehovah, they would have been offered in the name of Jesus. Perhaps some would have emphasised different aspects of Old Testament worship. For them the ritual/sacrifice side might be played down and greater emphasis given to the celebratory aspects of singing, dancing, offering worship to God in acts of praise. In both cases the emphasis is on what *we do* for God.

But the early Christians didn't go down either of these routes.

However, such descriptions do fit the way some churches operate today.

BC Today

On the one hand, there are the various forms of the Catholic movement with the priest in his vestments, offering the sacrifice of the mass on the altar to remove sins, with incense being wafted to create an atmosphere of mystery denoting a God who is hidden and unapproachable, except by the holy man. This is in effect Old Testament religion in New Testament guise.

On the other hand, there are certain strands of the charismatic movement. Here the one indispensable mediator is the worship leader, who, through the medium of music, creates the right atmosphere whereby we are prepared for 'worship'. In some cases God is bidden to come amongst his people, by an invocation of the Holy Spirit. To some extent this is reflected in the hymn, 'Jesus we enthrone you' and the words: 'Standing here in the midst of us, *we* raise you up with our praise. And as *we* worship build a throne . . .'. The worship (for which read praise) acts as an incantation to enable, or at least beseech, Jesus to build a throne. But the fact is, Jesus *is* enthroned and we are called to recognise that and respond to it.

Both developments might claim to be biblical, but they are only partly biblical in that they move too easily from the Old Testament to the present day without stopping to consider what has happened in between.

Why, then, didn't the early Christians do the most obvious thing and speak of worshipping at church, either through ritual or praise?

To answer that question we turn again to the Letter to the Hebrews which provides us with a detailed explanation why everything has changed with the coming of Jesus. By virtue of who he is and what he has done worship can never be the same again.

The Turning Point

All the important ideas you find in the Old Testament – sanctuary, sacrifice, altar, priesthood – are taken up by the writer and related to the person and work of Jesus. He is the one who has replaced the Old Testament – or Old Covenant – way of relating to God by a New Covenant, infinitely superior to, although clearly a development on, the Old Covenant. We read of this in chapter 9, verses 8–10: 'The Holy Spirit was showing by this that the way into the Most Holy Place had not yet been disclosed as long as the first tabernacle was still standing. This is an *illustration* for the present time, indicating that the gifts and sacrifices being offered were not able to clear the conscience of the worshipper. They are *only* a matter of food and drink and various ceremonial washings – external regulations applying until the time of the new order.' All these symbols were like visual aids pointing to a reality beyond themselves, but now that to which they were pointing has come: Jesus Christ.

We, therefore, find that Jesus is both the one great high priest and the one final sacrifice: God's final word and final work. 'In the past God spoke to our forefathers through the prophets at many times and in various ways, but in these last days he has spoken to us by his Son, whom he appointed heir of all things, and through whom he made the universe. . . . After he had provided purification for sins, he sat down at the right hand of the Majesty in heaven' (Heb. 1:1–3).

Jesus has dealt with our greatest problem, our sin, which separates us from a holy God by becoming the sacrifice for sin and so putting it away forever. All those things which trouble our conscience, those memories of moral failure that cause us to groan inwardly, God will not hold against us.

Jesus, we are told, has gone into the real holy of holies of which the earthly temple was a symbol: heaven itself (6:19; 9:11). As he does so he takes the Christian believer with him as it were. The reason why we don't need any earthly mediators (special 'holy' people, whether priests or worship leaders) to put us in touch with God is because Jesus is the one who brings us into contact with God directly (9:15). For those who trust in this great High Priest Son, believing his promises (4:14) they can draw near to God without religious rigmarole (10:19–23): 'Therefore, brothers, since we have confidence to enter the Most Holy Place by the blood of Jesus, by a new and living way opened for us through the curtain, that is, his body, and since we have a great priest over the house of God, let us draw near to God with a sincere heart in full assurance of faith, having our hearts sprinkled to cleanse us from a guilty conscience.'

The problem with BC Christian religion is that it is an attempt to take us back into the shadowlands of the Old Testament. AD Christianity brings us into the spiritual uplands which radiate with the sunshine of God's love. What faith in Jesus brings is not the formality and uncertainty of religion but the intimacy and assurance of a relationship – an engagement with God.

Why didn't the early church have a special priesthood? Because Jesus alone was their special priest. Why didn't they have any ritual as a sacrifice for sins? Because Jesus was the final sacrifice for sins. Why didn't they have special buildings which communicated the distance of God, having an altar, waving incense and all? Because through Jesus God has drawn near to us. Individually and corporately we are temples of the Holy Spirit – God dwelling in our midst – so we no longer have to go to special holy places, *we* are holy places ('Don't you know that you yourselves are God's temple and that God's Spirit lives in you?' – 1 Cor. 3:16). More than that, when Christians meet together on earth, *at the same* time they are brought into God's presence in heaven. Even as Christians meet as church in a building, although it cannot be seen with human eyes, they are being caught up in the worship of heaven: 'But you have come to Mount Zion, to the heavenly Jerusalem, the city of the living God. You have come to thousands upon thousands of angels in joyful assembly, to the church of the firstborn, whose names are written in heaven. You have come to God, the judge of all men, to the spirits of righteous men made perfect, to Jesus the mediator of a new covenant, and to the sprinkled blood that speaks a better word than the blood of Abel' (Heb. 12:22–4). Isn't that an amazing thought? That 'word' of which the writer speaks is the word of the Gospel; this is the promise that brings Christians together and ushers them into God's presence. To refuse this invitation in preference for man-made religion is to spurn God and bring judgement upon ourselves, as the writer goes on to spell out in verses 25ff: 'See to it that you do not refuse him who speaks. If they did not escape when they refused him who warned them on earth, how much less will we, if we turn away from him who warns us from heaven?'

Life as Worship

In the light of this unseen reality, the writer draws this conclusion in chapter 12, verse 28: 'Therefore, since we are receiving a kingdom that cannot be shaken, let us be thankful, and so worship God acceptably with reverence and awe, for our "God is a consuming fire." This inevitably raises the question: What worship or service to God *is* acceptable? Chapter 13 is really one long exposition of the answer, teasing out the practical implications of worship in *every* sphere of life. Worship is not just something we do when we meet together as church (although it includes that); it is something that embraces the whole of our lives as a result of what God has done for us in Jesus. He has saved us and made us his special people with a future hope and so we respond to God's love in serving him with gratitude – worship.

How?

In the first place, by entertaining strangers, being hospitable and visiting prisoners (vv. 1–3). Also by being

faithful in marriage and trusting God to provide for our
material needs, so refusing to be greedy (vv. 4–6). We
worship by imitating the faith of Christian leaders, holding on to good teaching and refusing to be led astray by
false religion with its emphasis on what we do for God
instead of responding gratefully for what he has done for
us (vv. 7–10). It means being willing to suffer as a
Christian, being treated with contempt as one 'outside
the camp' as happened to Jesus. When people are attack-
ing you for being a Christian and you stand firm, you are
actually worshipping God. True worship refuses to put
down roots in this world because those who worship the
living God know their real home is in heaven (vv. 11–13).
Certainly, those who have been freed from sin will offer
sacrifices of thanks and praise; that is, they will sing of
his glory even when they don't feel like it (v. 15). This
also includes witnessing – the 'confession of our lips'.
They will sacrifice time, effort and money to help those in
need. That is the sacrifice that really pleases God. It is far
more costly and far more valuable than ritual (v. 16).
Worship also involves hearing and obeying the word of
God, receiving the word ministry of teaching elders, not
the ministrations of sacrificing priests. It means not giving Christian leaders a difficult time, but making their
work a joy (v. 17). It also involves praying for Gospel
ministry and using the gifts that the Great Shepherd has
given us to encourage one another on in the faith
(vv. 20–1). We cannot get a more all-embracing and radical understanding of worship than this.

In many ways what we have been arguing in this
chapter is well summarised by Carson and Woodbridge
in their excellent book, *Letters along the Way*:

> The fundamental question to decide . . . is what worship
> is. At a rudimentary level, it is nothing but the ascription

of worth to God. But more can be said if we try to look
at the Biblical-theological structures that define a proper
approach to worship. . . . In the Old Testament, although
there is certainly a large place for private devotion, the
central place for worship is the temple and the entire
'cultic' apparatus which goes with it. Here one *serves* the
Lord and *worships* the Lord and *praises* the Lord. But
under the new covenant, it is astonishing how the 'cultic' terminology of the Old Testament is transmuted.
Christian worship is not associated with the temple, but
tied to all of Christian living. To go no farther than
Romans 12:1–2, our offering of ourselves to God is our
'spiritual worship.' This pattern (as several writers have
pointed out) is a constant feature of the New Testament
'worship' language (e.g., *leitourgia* and cognates, etc.) On
the other hand, the conclusion sometimes drawn from
this valid observation has missed the mark. It has been
argued that if Christian worship involves all of life, then
what we do when we come together for corporate meetings cannot properly be called 'worship'; it must be
something else. This 'something' has variously been
tagged fellowship, instruction, mutual exhortation, or
the like . . . It is surely better to argue that, just as our
entire life is to be lived out in worship to God in an attitude and a style and a faithfulness that is constantly
ascribing praise to Him and giving thanks to Him (after
all, the church can almost be defined as those everywhere who call on the name of the Lord, 1 Corinthians
1:2), so also our coming together is supremely marked
by such worship. In this view, the other things that enter
into our services are part of worship. It is not that we
worship for a few minutes (for instance, in singing) and
then have a time of sharing that cannot be considered
worship or listen to a sermon that should be dubbed
'instruction' but not 'worship.' Rather, all that we do in

our corporate meetings, as in all our lives when we are
on our own, must be offered up to God as an offering to
Him, a service, worship. We are doing corporately and
with total concentration what we should have been
doing on our own all week – we are worshipping the living God' (p. 251).

First and foremost, then, worship is a result of God moving towards us in love through his Word, which includes
the symbols of baptism and the Lord's Supper, which
picture the Gospel for us. Then there is the upward
movement in praise and prayer as we respond to God's
love in Jesus. But there is also the outward movement
towards one another and the world as we show acts of
kindness and share the Gospel, so that others may also
be embraced by divine love: this is worship.

So let the question be posed again: Are you a BC
Christian or an AD Christian? The answer makes all the
difference in the world.

9

Prayer in the Church
Acts 4:23–31

On their release, Peter and John went back to their own people and reported all that the chief priests and elders had said to them. When they heard this, they raised their voices together in prayer to God. 'Sovereign Lord,' they said, 'you made the heaven and the earth and the sea, and everything in them. You spoke by the Holy Spirit through the mouth of your servant, our father David:

*"Why do the nations rage
and the peoples plot in vain?
The kings of the earth take their stand
and the rulers gather together
against the Lord
and against his Anointed One."*

Indeed Herod and Pontius Pilate met together with the Gentiles and the people of Israel in this city to conspire against your holy servant Jesus, whom you anointed. They did what your power and will had decided beforehand should happen. Now, Lord, consider their threats and enable your servants to speak your word with great boldness. Stretch out your hand to heal and perform miraculous signs and wonders through the name of your holy servant Jesus.'

After they prayed, the place where they were meeting was shaken. And they were all filled with the Holy Spirit and spoke the word of God boldly.

The scene is an old Spanish mission station in the middle of a desert. Tumbleweed is blowing around, and the odd dog is lying in the dust. Standing in front of it is a monk with a tonsured haircut, wearing a coarse brown robe, which makes you itch just looking at it, with a piece of rope around the middle. His hands are clasped prayerfully in front of him, and he looks meek and fragile, unworldly, unsophisticated and undernourished, probably from fasting. He stands before two big horses, and sitting on those horses are the Lone Ranger and his trusty companion Tonto. The horses look ready for action with their flared nostrils and hooves pawing at the ground. The Lone Ranger and Tonto have their guns drawn, and their faces are fixed in grim determination. The monk says: 'I want to go with you.' 'You're a brave man, Father,' the Lone Ranger replies, 'but it may be dangerous. You had better stay here where it is safe.' 'But I want to help,' the monk says. 'I suppose you could pray,' replies the Lone Ranger. At that moment, his great white horse rears up on its hind legs and with a wave of his hat and hearty 'Heigh Ho Silver – Away!' the Lone Ranger and his trusty companion disappear into the distance to wrestle with danger and the forces of evil, while the monk is left to pray in safety. Be honest, who would you prefer to go with? The Lone Ranger and Tonto, or the monk? For most of us, it would be the Lone Ranger, because we believe that is where the action will be.

Being honest, that is what many of us often feel about prayer. It seems so weak and helpless on the face of it. It certainly doesn't look like that is where the excitement is to be found. We would much prefer to be doing things than spending time in prayer. And there is no doubt that in our increasingly busy lives, prayer gets squeezed. But when we turn to look at the early Christian church, we discover something else. Prayer for them was right at the heart of their corporate lives, their life together as a church. And they were one of the most exciting churches ever!

We get a snippet of what it was like in Acts, chapter 4. This is an incredible chapter. Peter and John have been arrested for healing a cripple and for teaching the crowds about Jesus. But when they are brought before the authorities, they give such a good account of themselves that the police don't know what to do with them. So they let them off with a stern warning, and a threat of physical violence. But when they go back to their church family they pray a most astonishing prayer. On the face of it, that is a very strange thing to do. It looks so weak. If we were one of them no doubt we would be tempted to take on the authorities, rather like the Lone Ranger and Tonto. But they don't. They pray. The reason is because they are a God-centred church. They know the secret of success and that is to humble themselves before their God and pray. In our impatient, active, pushy society, we have much to learn from this first church. In the Bible the real action is where people are praying. When the tough get going, the people get praying! And what shaped and galvanised their praying was their theocentricity – everything was *God*-centred.

God-Centred Priorities

The first thing we discover is that their priorities were thoroughly God-centred. Verse 23: 'On their release,

Peter and John went back to their own people and reported all that the chief priests had said to them.' The beautiful thing about this verse is that we discover that the leaders went straight back to their own people after they had been released from prison. This church was obviously so loving that they felt right at home among their fellow Christians. These people had become their spiritual brothers and sisters, their new-found family. That in itself is a challenge! It was in that loving family environment that these leaders told what had happened. What was their gut-reaction to this news? Verse 24: 'When they heard this, they raised their voices together in prayer to God.' Their immediate reflex-reaction was to pray! They didn't form a committee, nor did they write a letter of complaint to the Chief Superintendent. They prayed. What is more, this was something the whole church were involved in. They raised their voices *together*. In so doing they showed exactly what their priorities were.

In their immediate reaction they showed where they believed the real authority and source of power was. They knew that they must humble themselves before their God and commit this situation to him. They showed their utter dependency upon God for everything. It is quite clear when we read Scripture that God expects his people to pray. Jesus assumed his disciples would pray and he taught them how to do it. He said, in the Sermon on the Mount: '*When* you pray...' not 'if you pray'. Paul asks his supporting churches to pray for him. Paul himself gives many models of prayers he prays for people he is concerned with. Obviously we don't know the mechanics of how God answers prayer. We are just told that he does. He really does use human prayers for his work. William Temple, when challenged that so-called answers to prayer were mere coincidences, replied: 'The funny thing is, when I pray coincidences happen. When I don't the coincidences stop!' Time and again in Scripture God answers the prayers of his people, and he expects his people to pray to him. In fact, one writer has suggested that prayerlessness is actually a sin, because we are effectively telling God that we can handle things on our own by our attitude of not praying. But not this church. They know that they *must* pray. Prayer was right at the heart of all they did as a church together. They put prayer at the top of their church agenda, and it revealed their God-centred priorities.

The question that we need to ask ourselves is whether prayer is *our* natural reaction. Is it the natural reaction of a church? Because our attitude to prayer reveals our priorities. If it is something we cannot be bothered with, then it shows we are content to live life our way, with never a thought for God and his ways. We show we are self-sufficient. It is a great pity that the central church meeting, if there is one at all, still tends to be the most neglected meeting of the week. It should not be so. They are meant to be great times where Christians as a body gather together, like this early church, to pray and ask God to strengthen them for the fight, to be at work in all that is done. There is to be that showing of a dependency on him. If we learn little else from the example of the early church, let us learn this, to put prayer at the top of our agenda in gathering together.

God-Centred Understanding

Secondly, we discover that they had a God-centred understanding. A God-centred understanding of what? Of God himself! Notice who it is they pray to in verse 24. They pray to the *sovereign Lord*. In other words, they knew the God to whom they were praying. They understood this amazing truth about him that he is sovereign, and it radically affected the way they prayed and what they prayed for. God's sovereignty means all God's majestic and kingly qualities, his ability to rule and to direct the universe as he wants. He is the God who is in control, he is the Lord and no one can thwart his plans. The early church knew they were praying to a God like that.

First, they saw that he was *Lord over creation*. Verse 24: 'You made the heaven and the earth and the sea, and everything in them.' God exercised his amazing rule and authority even over the very creation itself. There is nothing that God does not control. The interesting thing about this verse is that it is a direct quotation from a prayer that had been prayed several hundred years before. It came from a prayer of King Hezekiah who was king over Judah in Isaiah's time when Jerusalem was being threatened by the Assyrians under King Sennacharib. Isaiah tells the whole story in chapters 36–8 of his prophecy. When Hezekiah heard about the news of the impending attack by the Assyrians, he prayed to the Lord, and he started off by praising God for his sovereignty, his lordship over creation. In the face of a massive invasion and a seemingly no-win situation, Hezekiah prayed to the only God who had the power to help in that situation. What happened? The Assyrians were miraculously destroyed and Jerusalem was spared. It was to this same powerful God, who ruled the heavens and the earth and everything in them, that this first church prayed, facing a similar no-win situation with the authorities against them. They too trusted in God's amazing sovereignty. So if this God ruled the heavens, then he would certainly make quick work of any human rulers. Do you see how comforting this doctrine is? This

God that we believe in is so incredibly powerful it is almost incredible. When we pray we are speaking to this powerful God.

On 20 August 1977, Voyager II, the inter-planetary probe launched to observe and transmit to earth data about the outer planetary system, set off from earth travelling at 90,000 miles an hour, faster than a speeding bullet. On the 28 August 1989, over ten years later, it reached Neptune, some 2,700 million miles from earth. Voyager II then left the solar system. It will not come within one light year of any star for another 958,000 years, give or take ten years. In our galaxy there are 100,000 million stars like our sun. Our galaxy is one of at least 100,000 million galaxies. That invariably makes you feel small, but also incredible privileged and special! The writer of Genesis casually mentions that among other things God made the stars. It is a mind-blowing truth. Do we really even begin to understand who we are praying to? That first church did. He was the Lord of creation.

But he's also the *Lord over history*. Verse 25: 'You spoke by the Holy Spirit through the mouth of your servant, our father David: "Why do the nations rage and the peoples plot in vain? The kings of the earth take their stand and the rulers gather against the Lord and against his Anointed One."' In its prayer this church includes a quotation from Psalm 2. It was well known that this was a messianic Psalm – a psalm that talked about Jesus, the Messiah. It is interesting to note that this church recognised that God was the ultimate author of scripture, for even though David wrote the Psalm, nonetheless it was the Holy Spirit who spoke through the mouth of David. What did David say? He said that 'the nations rage and the peoples plot in vain. The kings of the earth take their stand and the rulers gather together against the Lord and against his Anointed One.' And sure enough that was what happened. When the Messiah did come, he was conspired against. And this church sees in Jesus' crucifixion a fulfilment of this Psalm. The rulers and the kings and the nations and the people are all seen in real life. There is Herod, Pilate, the Gentile Romans and the people of Israel. But the amazing thing is that it was all part of God's plan. 'They did what your power and will had decided beforehand should happen' (v. 28). So there were these people thinking they had got rid of this pest Jesus, when all along they were doing exactly what God had planned in eternity. God is never taken by surprise. No one can thwart his plans. He is in control of history. People will be held responsible for their actions. They have done terrible things that they might have appeared to have got away with, but they will never get one over on God. He is the sovereign Lord of history. In verse 4 of Psalm 2, just after the verses quoted in Acts 4, the psalmist writes that 'the One enthroned in heaven laughs [at these rulers who oppose God]; the Lord scoffs at them.' There they are shaking their puny fists at God, and he just laughs at them. You cannot outsmart the God of the universe, the God of history itself.

Do you see now why these people were so bold in their prayers, why the first thing they did was to pray? Because they knew the God they prayed to. Perhaps we might want to ask ourselves how we can *not* pray to a God so awesomely powerful and supreme? Should we ever doubt that he will fulfil his purposes?

God doesn't always answer perhaps how we would like him to, but we can be absolutely assured that his purposes for us are the absolute best. And we can trust him completely because he's the God of creation and the God of history.

God-Centred Request

In the third place we come to what they actually prayed for and we discover a God-centred request: 'Now, Lord, consider their threats and enable your servants to speak your word with great boldness. Stretch out your hand to perform miraculous signs and wonders through the name of your holy servant Jesus' (v. 29).

What would we have prayed in this situation with the authorities breathing down our necks? 'Lord, come down in judgement upon those who oppose you and us?' Maybe. 'Lord, please stop this persecution that is happening.' Probably. But would we have prayed for boldness to speak out? It seems almost insane! Apart from the fact that it is right! 'Enable your servants to speak your word with great boldness.' What was the most important thing that could have happened in Jerusalem? The most important thing that could have happened was that the Gospel would be preached, despite the suffering. And so this early church prayed for exactly that. They were praying in line with what they knew God wanted and what would bring God and his Son glory. They knew that was the most important thing. They didn't pray with selfish agendas, they prayed with gospel agendas, God's agenda in line with God's revealed will. They knew full well that they were to preach the gospel. So, they prayed, 'Lord give us the boldness to do it. Equip us for the task you have given us to do.' It would seem that the reason they prayed for signs and wonders to happen was that they were authenticating signs of the power of the Gospel. In the Bible miraculous signs are often clustered around big events of revelation like the time of Moses, Elijah, and Jesus and the early church. They are, if you like, big sign-posts to what God is doing. But even at these times, the word of the Gospel is by far the most important thing. Today that should be our main emphasis as it was for the disciples, however much we may believe these things happen today.

But then see how God answered their prayer. The meeting place is shaken as a sign of God's presence; they are filled with the Holy Spirit; and they speak the Word of God boldly. We are to take note of something vitally important here. *God himself* is at work in them. That's what it means to be filled with the Holy Spirit. Paul makes it clear in Ephesians 5 that this is to be an ongoing experience; that the more we grow as Christians, the more Christ-like we become and the more we walk the Spirit's way. We need a work of God's Spirit to equip us to serve him. Very few of us are natural evangelists. But each of us who is a Christian has the Spirit of God in us. So we need to pray that he would equip us and embolden us for the task.

How often do we pray prayers like that? We might well wonder sometimes if the reason some of our prayers are not answered is because we are not praying the right things. If you examine the prayers of Scripture, they are always praying things which will bring God glory, rather than enhancing the good of the prayer. Studying the prayers of Paul is an excellent way to see the sorts of things we ought to be praying for one another. Paul's requests, like this church's, were always God-centred requests. How about ours? If we are honest, how many of our prayers are *self*-centred?

Here is a prayer written in the eighteenth century by a man called John Ward of Hackney. It's a classic example of man-centred praying: 'O Lord, thou knowest that I have nine estates in the City of London, and likewise that I have lately purchased one estate in the county of Essex; I beseech thee to preserve the two counties of

Essex and Middlesex from fire and earthquake; and as I have a mortgage in Hertfordshire, I beg of thee likewise to have an eye of compassion on that county. As for the rest of the counties, thou mayest deal with them as thou art pleased. O Lord, enable the bank to answer their bills, and make all my debtors good men. Give a prosperous voyage and return to the Mermaid ship, as I have insured her.' This is hardly praying for God's glory. But how would our prayers stand up? Let's take a leaf out of this church's book, and pray God-centred requests.

Having looked at this prayer of that early Christian gathering, where would you rather be? In the saddle next to the Lone Ranger, or back at the ranch praying? Hopefully we have caught a glimpse of why being back at the ranch is actually more exciting, for we are praying to the God of the universe, the one who holds the very keys of history. Does that excite you? It did these people. They had God-centred priorities, having prayer at the top of their agenda; they had a God-centred understanding of God and his sovereignty, and they prayed God-centred requests, not wanting their own glory but His. May God enable us to pray more like them.

10

The Influence of the Church
Matthew 5:13–16

You are the light of the world. A city on a hill cannot be hidden. Neither do people light a lamp and put it under a bowl. Instead they put it on its stand, and it gives light to everyone in the house. In the same way, let your light shine before men, that they may see your good deeds and praise your Father in heaven.

There is an ancient Greek myth that tells of a goddess who came to earth unseen but whose presence was always known by the blessings she left behind in her pathway. Trees burned by forest fires sprouted new leaves, and violets sprang up in her footprints. As she passed a stagnant pool its water became fresh, and parched fields turned green as she walked through them. Hills and valleys blossomed with new life and beauty wherever she went. It is an enchanting story. It also captures something of the effect the followers of Jesus, his church, should have in the world in which he has placed them. These words which follow the characteristics of Jesus' 'happy' or 'blessed' people, spell out just what influence for the good they are meant to have.

The obvious question is, 'What kind of influence can such people have in the world? They look so weak and feeble.' Jesus' answer is that his followers *are* salt and light in the world, not that they should be. They can and should have a profound influence for good.

The fact of the matter is that in God's plan the people who have been transformed by the power of the gospel and who are living lives marked by the qualities of verses 1–12 are to have a role in penetrating the world with the life-changing message of God. This message must be lived out by Jesus' followers in the world. Jesus never expects such qualities to be lived out in cosy communities, like little churchy salt cellars or nice, warm light shops. No, Christians are to be in the world, being, as Jesus says, salt and light. That is what they are. It is not a tough option for the keen Christians. It is the command of the Lord Jesus for all Christians. We are salt and light, and by definition salt is for putrid meat, and light is for dark places. It is a task that the whole church together is to be devoted to. You (plural) says Jesus, are the salt of the earth; you (plural) are the light of the world. Thankfully only a few of us are paid to be full-time pastors and teachers. For the rest of us, we will be in the world working and living and interacting with those who are not Christians. The church, if you like, is a giant octopus with its tentacles finding its way into all sorts of areas where Christians work and spend their time. And it is in those places that the Christian church, represented by individual Christians, are to be salt and light.

Jesus' words offer all Christians down the ages three challenges.

Understand the World

First, we must understand the world in which we live. Jesus says that we are the salt of the earth and the light

of the world. The unflattering assumption that Jesus
gives in these verses is that the world is a decaying,
putrid and dark place. Salt in the ancient world, and
indeed still sometimes today, was used as a preservative.
In days when there were no fridges and freezers, salt
would be used to stop food going off. It would be
rubbed into meat, for example, or used to stop fish
rotting by packing them into mounds of salt. The
assumption is that the world is like that fish or meat. It
is rotting away, and it needs the protection of salt to keep
it from decaying any faster. Of course, salt won't stop
the rot completely, but it will drastically slow the rot. Or
take the next verse about light. The assumption here is
that the world is a dark place. You don't need lights in a
lighted room; only where it is dark and dingy do you
need the warm glow of a lamp. Jesus says that this world
needs Christians to be in it to slow the rot and shine in
the darkness.

It has to be admitted that Jesus' assessment of the
world goes against the grain. Few would say that
the world is slowly rotting away, morally, physically and
spiritually. Many would say the world isn't in great
shape, but not that many would be so severe in their
assessment. A good number would point to the great
advances in technology that have been seen in recent
years, the great leaps and bounds we have made in
health care, the way food production has been enhanced
. . . so that we have butter mountains and milk lakes and
the like. Many would rejoice that God has been pushed
out of the picture in the western world because of the so-
called Enlightenment. We are living in the post-
Christian age, we are told. And yet is it a new dawn? Is
our world so wonderful? Two-thirds of the world do not
have enough to eat, despite the huge resources we in the
west have. In many of our major cities there is rising

violent crime, increasing teenage pregnancy, spiralling divorce rates and no end of broken hearts. The long-established moral framework that our parents instilled in us is being whittled away. Let us be realistic: we live in a rotting and dark world.

Perhaps one of the most graphic illustrations of this is seen in the film *Good Morning Vietnam*, starring Robin Williams. Williams plays an American forces DJ, and in one particular scene he is playing a record by Louis Armstrong, 'What a Wonderful World'. As the camera pans round, it moves from the studio to the world outside. There are scenes of napalm exploding, children being burnt alive, whole villages being destroyed, and as we watch the pictures, Louis Armstrong sings on: 'I see trees of green and skies of blue . . . and I say to myself what a wonderful world.' Yes, the world is a very wonderful place, but our experience shows that it is also a place of terrible evil and suffering. That is Jesus' assumption in these verses. The world, for all its beauty and for all God's goodness to mankind, is slowly decaying and is becoming darker and darker.

It is vitally important that we grasp the seriousness of the situation. For only then can we administer the correct medicine of the Gospel of Jesus Christ to this sick world. We need to understand our world.

Slow the Rot

Once we have understood the world in all its rot and darkness, then we can understand the challenge before us: as Christians we are meant to slow the rot. That is what Jesus means when he says in verse 13: 'You are the salt of the earth.' It would be very easy to get depressed looking at our world. Yet there is hope. And here's the surprise. That hope is you and me – followers of Christ! There is a very sharp distinction between the church and the world, which is sinful humanity opposed to God. It is to the church that Jesus gives this command: 'You are the salt of the earth.' You who are the meek and the peacemakers and persecuted, yes, you are to be the salt of the earth. Incredible isn't it? What does Jesus actually mean?

As we have already seen, salt in the ancient world was used as a preservative. It slowed the rotting of food. It is as if Jesus is saying to us that we Christians are the ones who have been given the task of slowing the rot in the world. We are, if you will, the moral disinfectant for the world in which we live. We have God's morality and truth, and so Jesus says live it out in the world and slow the rot which is taking place. Rub yourself into the flesh of the world and get involved. Stand up for biblical ideals and show a better way.

It is highly unlikely that Jesus is asking you to go into your office on Monday morning, stand on a desk and say: 'Woe to you heathen, woe to the evils that you have done on Saturday night at that club'! Judgement must be left to God alone. Sometimes of course it may be right to denounce something. Often this will take place in the public realm. Institutions like the Christian Institute and CARE take a very public stand on issues such as homosexuality or human rights. They are being salt in the public sphere, pointing out something that is wrong, and suggesting in its place something that is right. We should support that work, perhaps lobbying our MP about the age of consent, showing that the agenda of certain pressure groups is not the only one available. Christians down the years have always got involved in the public sphere and we have seen many wonderful successes for the promotion of biblical ideals. We only have to mention people like William Wilberforce, Lord Shaftsbury, Dr Barnado, George Muller and others. They were Christians who acted as salt in the public realm and were able to make big changes. And how we need men and women like that today. We should pray for Christians in parliament that they would be salt, slowing the rot by promoting God's values. Sir Fred Catherwood, former MEP and President of the Evangelical Alliance, has said that: 'To try to improve society is not worldliness but love. To wash your hands of society is not love but worldliness.' We should certainly be praying for friends involved in the media that they would be salt in those rotting places. Christians must be seen to be taking a stand in this public realm.

But most of us are not in the public sphere. How are we to be the salt of the earth? More often than not, being salt means not so much *saying* anything, as *being* something. In other words, the quality of our lives is to be the way we show our saltiness. We are to live lives which are distinctive from the world around us, putting into practice those Gospel qualities which Jesus talks about in verses 1–12. Take for instance the woman or man that works in the office. She tries not to swear, and she doesn't get involved in the backbiting that often happens when the boss' back is turned, and when the dirty jokes are flying around, she quietly slips away to get a cup of coffee because it's clear that they make her feel uncomfortable. She never makes a big thing of it, and she wouldn't have a go at the others, but she just doesn't get involved. She tries to say a warm hello to the receptionist each morning, and she remembers when her colleague's mother has to go into hospital so she can ask how she is. She works hard and tries not to complain. She tries not to put people down when she is tired or overworked. And over time people begin to notice.

Some don't like it; Jesus of course said in verse 13 that we will be persecuted. Salt does bite. But others secretly respect her. Some will even stop swearing because they know she doesn't like it.

You may think we are describing 'Samantha the Super Christian', but actually all this lady is doing (and there are plenty like her who do it), is applying the teaching of the Bible to the workplace, not in some superspiritual show off sort of way, and certainly by not being judgemental, but in a way that is humble and gracious. She loves her Lord and she wants to be salt in that office. She is living a life that is distinct from those around her.

But notice too that there is a warning. Jesus says that 'if the salt loses its saltiness, how can it be made salty again? It is no longer good for anything, except to be thrown out and trampled by men.' Strictly speaking salt cannot lose its saltiness. But what often happened in the ancient world was that salt would be mixed up with other impurities, so that the salt itself would be leeched out, leaving just a mushy white mess. All it was fit for was to be chucked out. Jesus is not teaching us chemistry; he is making a very serious theological point. If we are not being salty and distinctive in the world in which we live and work, then we are as good as tasteless white mush. We are as good as the rotting and putrid world around us. In fact the word for 'lose its saltiness' literally means to be a fool. A foolish Christian has no impact in the world. The Christian who goes with the flow in the office, who swears like the best, who backbites with the rest and whose lifestyle at the leaving do's and end of year parties leaves a lot to be desired, is fit for nothing according to Jesus. They have lost their saltiness. They too are like putrid and rotting fish. Fit for nothing except to be thrown out. That is

Jesus' warning. Don't be conformed to the world around you. Be distinct: be salty.

There's an old Greek story about a man called Jason who sailed to discover the Golden Fleece with a crew of sailors called the Argonauts. One day they sailed past an island on which were some creatures called Sirens who were half woman and half beast. But they had beautiful voices and they used to lure passing ships to their island and then kill them. Jason knew this danger and as they were passing the island Jason sang his own crew a song. The crew had a choice. To listen to Jason's song and be saved or else to listen to the song of the Sirens and risk jumping overboard to go to the island and face certain death. And there are two voices ringing in our ears all the time. Jesus' voice in His Word, or the voice of the world. The voice of the master teacher Jesus is saying 'Listen to me. Be distinctive. Be salty. If not then you are heading for disaster.'

Spread the Light

The final challenge is to spread the light. Verse 14: 'You are the light of the world.' If the challenge of the previous verse was don't lose it, then the challenge of this verse is don't hide it. Both salt and light are complementary. Salt has the negative effect of slowing the rot; but light has the positive effect of pointing the way and bringing light to darkness. The interesting thing is that Jesus does not say you are the honey of the world. Rather he said you are salt and light. We are not just in the world to be sweet and nice. Rather we are in the world to be distinct and point the way to Jesus. It is the latter half that Jesus is teaching us now. For it is not enough simply to be different. People need to know *why* we are different. The answer comes in where we get our light from. Jesus himself is the light of the world and we reflect his light. For example when you look at the moon, you don't actually see the moon shining on a bright night; what you see is light reflected from the sun. And so the Christian reflects Jesus' light, the light of the Son of God. We are light, and so we must point people to the light that is Jesus. We are not simply nicer people than the rest in the office. Rather we follow a Lord who has set a different standard, a Lord who has paid the ultimate price to get us out of this dark and rotting world, a Lord who longs for others to come to him too. We are the means to lead others to him. We are lights who point to the light.

Of course, a big temptation is to conceal that light, to hide the real reason why we are different. Many of us can testify to lost opportunities whereby someone has perhaps asked why we are different or what makes us tick, and we squirmed and wriggled and then eventually said something wishy washy and vague. Let us not wallow in the guilt, rather let us keep asking God to give us those opportunities and to have the courage to take them when they come. We have nothing to be ashamed of.

Jesus gives two illustrations of what we are to be like. We are to be like a city on a hill. You can see it for miles around; it cannot be hidden. So too the Christian who is being truly salty in the world. Nor do you hide a lamp under your bed. No, you put it on a lampstand so that it shines for all to see. Don't hide that light, says Jesus. You are there for a reason, to point people to me. The German pastor Dietrich Bonhoeffer once said these words: 'Flight into the invisible is a denial of the call [to be a Christian]. A community of Jesus which seeks to hide itself has ceased to follow him.' God really wants to use us in the world where we are. That is our mission field. Don't hide the light.

Notice the way this happens. Verse 16: 'In the same way, let your light shine before men that they might see your good deeds and praise your father in heaven.' Again it is the *life* you lead which is so effective. Jesus says that some non-Christians will end up glorifying God because of our witness. We are like shop windows. People can look at us and see, imperfectly maybe, the light of Christ. It is not we who get the glory but God. This does happen. I know of someone, we shall call her Jill, who knew a girl who was not a Christian at university. They lived on the same corridor together in a set of flats. Over those years this girl saw Jill's life, and on just a few occasions Jill was able to tell her about Jesus. They both left university and a couple of years later Jill received a letter from this girl. The letter was amazing. It said that she had become a Christian, and then she said these words. 'I looked at your life and I saw something different. I realised that there was something special about you, and I just had to investigate.' That investigation led her to Christ. Jill had reflected Jesus' light. Don't hide it, says Jesus. You *are* the light of the world.

We may not be Greek goddesses, but we are meant to give evidence of authentic Christianity in our day-to-day lives, individually and corporately. It is the Christian's privilege and responsibility. It won't always be easy, but it is what we are called to do. Hear the challenge: Don't lose it and don't hide it. For you are the salt of the earth and the light of the world.

11

The Future of the Church
Revelation 21

Then I saw a new heaven and a new earth, for the first heaven and the first earth had passed away, and there was no longer any sea. I saw the Holy City, the new Jerusalem, coming down out of heaven from God, prepared as a bride beautifully dressed for her husband. And I heard a loud voice from the throne saying, 'Now the dwelling of God is with men, and he will live with them. They will be his people, and God himself will be with them and be their God. He will wipe every tear from their eyes. There will be no more death or mourning or crying or pain, for the old order of things has passed away.'

He who was seated on the throne said, 'I am making everything new!' Then he said, 'Write this down, for these words are trustworthy and true.'

He said to me: 'It is done. I am the Alpha and the Omega, the Beginning and the End. To him who is thirsty I will give to drink without cost from the spring of the water of life. He who overcomes will inherit all this, and I will be his God and he will be my son. But the cowardly, the unbelieving, the vile, the murderers, the sexually immoral, those who practice magic arts, the idolaters and all liars-their place will be in the fiery lake of burning sulfur. This is the second death.'

One of the seven angels who had the seven bowls full of the seven last plagues came and said to me, 'Come, I will show you the bride, the wife of the Lamb.' And he carried me away in the Spirit to a mountain great and high, and showed me the Holy City, Jerusalem, coming down out of heaven from God. It shone with the glory of God, and its brilliance was like that of a very precious jewel, like a jasper, clear as crystal. It had a great, high wall with twelve gates, and with twelve angels at the gates. On the gates were written the names of the twelve tribes of Israel. There were three gates on the east, three on the north, three on the south and three on the west. The wall of the city had twelve foundations, and on them were the names of the twelve apostles of the Lamb.

The angel who talked with me had a measuring rod of gold to measure the city, its gates and its walls. The city was laid out like a square, as long as it was wide. He measured the city with the rod and found it to be 12,000 stadia in length, and as wide and high as it is long. He measured its wall and it was 144 cubits thick, by man's measurement, which the angel was using. The wall was made of jasper, and the city of pure gold, as pure as glass. The foundations of the city walls were decorated with every kind of precious stone. The first foundation was jasper, the second sapphire, the third chalcedony, the fourth emerald, the fifth sardonyx, the sixth carnelian, the seventh chrysolite, the eighth beryl, the ninth topaz, the tenth chrysoprase, the eleventh jacinth, and the twelfth amethyst. The twelve gates were twelve pearls, each gate made of a single pearl. The great street of the city was of pure gold, like transparent glass.

I did not see a temple in the city, because the Lord God Almighty and the Lamb are its temple. The city does not need the sun or the moon to shine on it, for the glory of God gives it light, and the Lamb is its lamp. The nations will walk by its

*light, and the kings of the earth will bring their splendor into
it. On no day will its gates ever be shut, for there will be no
night there. The glory and honor of the nations will be brought
into it. Nothing impure will ever enter it, nor will anyone who
does what is shameful or deceitful, but only those whose names
are written in the Lamb's book of life.*

Heaven tends not have a good press these days. The
writer Laurie Lee had this to say about it: 'Heaven is too
chaste, too disinfected, too much on its best behaviour. It
receives little more than a dutiful nod from the faithful.
Hell, on the other hand, is always a good crowd-raiser,
having ninety percent of the action – high colours, high
temperatures, intricate devilries, and always the most
interesting company available.' But then again, the alternative doesn't seem that appealing either; the belief that
this life is all there is and after it there is nothing. So
writes Bertrand Russell: 'There is a darkness without
and when I die there will be a darkness within. There is
no splendour, no vastness anywhere, only triviality for a
moment and then nothing.' As a race we are in short
supply of what the Bible calls 'hope'. Not the vague
'hoping against hope' which breezily enjoins us always
to look on the bright side of life no matter how much the
odds are stacked against us. But rather the quiet, assured
knowledge that the One who made this world will bring
it to a good, just and satisfying goal, and that central to
all of God's plans and purposes for his entire universe is
his church.

One of the most stunning passages in the whole of
the Bible, which uses picture-laden language to help
us to catch a glimpse of what God has in store for those
who love him, is Revelation 21. This presents us with
the perfection of what every true church of Jesus
Christ now experiences partially. The church is meant

to be a place of real community; a gathering in which people experience true intimacy; a people where needs are met and there is sufficiency; a group distinguishable from the world by its purity and a folk who know that their ultimate security is in God whatever may come their way.

What's new?

'Then I saw a new heaven and a new earth, for the first heaven and the first earth had passed away, and there was no longer any sea' (v. 1). 'He who was seated on the throne said, "I am making everything new!" ' (v. 5).

What God has in view is a brand new replacement for this universe of ours. It is still a physical universe – a heaven and earth – but it is 'new', that is, a new *kind* of universe. To begin with, there will not be anything in it that is dark, chaotic and rebellious. That is what is meant by that intriguing little phrase: 'There was no longer any sea'; that is not a comment on the hydrology of the world to come, so if you like a day at the seaside don't worry! It is simply that the sea in Scripture symbolises all the dark turmoil which characterises this present fallen order of things – the Bosnias, the Hiroshimas. Or we might think of it this way: the world as we experience it at the moment will be transfigured into something which, quiet frankly, is infinitely more wonderful, more fascinating and more intricate and beautiful than anything we can possibly imagine within the confines of our present space and time. Even the most creative novelist in the world could not even begin to dream of one fraction of this world which Jesus Christ will one day usher into existence. That, in part, is what the following imagery is meant to communicate to us.

But what really lies behind the symbolism of this passage is not speculation about the colour of the grass of heaven, but the heart of the nature of heaven which is all to do with *relationships*.

Home from Home

We discover that the first promise is that God's people, his church, will experience *real community*: 'I saw the Holy City, the new Jerusalem, coming down out of heaven from God, prepared as a bride beautifully dressed for her husband' (v. 2). We are not to be confused by the fact that John mixes his symbols, by speaking of the city as *also* being a bride. That is the way this kind of literature, called apocalyptic, works. We are dealing with pictures that convey marvellous truths of eternity, not architectural drawings of heaven. And that we have a mixing of symbols at this point should alert us to the fact that what we have here is simply an alternative way of thinking about the new heaven and new earth in their entirety. In other words it is describing the same thing in different ways: a renewed and redeemed universe.

What do we see? It is a city. A city, as we know, is a dwelling place for people, a community where there is friendship and activity; where people work together, live together, even celebrate together, which of course is also what happens at a wedding with the bride – there is a joyful family gathering. What is more, this is a *holy City*, distinguishable from any other city in the world: pure, unsullied, with everything functioning properly. Notice too that it is called the new Jerusalem: this is *God's* city, the unrivalled city of peace. Furthermore it comes *down* from heaven. Here we have a contrast to

Babel, a symbol of man's arrogance and pride in trying to construct the perfect city, reaching up *to* heaven, by himself (Gen. 11). When we try to do that, by cutting God out of the picture and acting like little gods ourselves, we do not create heaven on earth, but hell on earth. Hitler's Berlin, Stalin's Stalingrad, Nebuchadnezzar's Babylon were built on the broken backs of thousands of people in oppression and despair. Our cities now tend to be rather dark places, lonely places, even dangerous places. But God's city, coming down from heaven as a gift, is full of light: 'The city does not need the sun or the moon to shine on it, for the glory of God gives it light, and the Lamb is its lamp' (v. 23) This city overcomes loneliness by bringing people together in joyous celebration. Again, the wedding symbolism is important here. It is at weddings that families and friends are brought together. As you meet it is as if the years have all fallen away and you have never been apart. Indeed, it is as if something of the love of the bride and groom spill over and all the guests are caught up in it. But we shall all be the bride on that day, the focus of the adoring gaze of our husband, the Lord Jesus. This means that we shall meet again those whom we love and who have died in Christ. The frustration death brings, as we long to go back in time to meet with that father or husband, child or wife, just to see them again and talk with them for a few moments – all of that will be overcome in this city. The sadness of the funeral is replaced by the mirth of the wedding.

This brings us to the second heart-melting feature of the nature of the glorified church: *perfect intimacy*. 'And I heard a loud voice from the throne saying, 'Now the dwelling of God is with men, and he will live with them. They will be his people, and God himself will be with them and be their God. He will wipe every tear from their eyes. There will be no more death or mourning or crying or pain, for the old order of things has passed away' (v. 3). Remember the promise of Jesus: 'Where two or three are gathered together in my name, there I am in their midst'? That is a reality whenever God's people meet together on earth as church. But that is also the ultimate reality we shall all experience in heaven. *We* shall be the dwelling place of God. God will be with his people. That was his original purpose when he created the universe as we see it in the Book of Genesis. God walked with Adam in the garden of Eden, talking with him, sharing with him, but on that great day the intimacy we shall experience will be much deeper than anything Adam could ever have dreamt of: 'They will be his people, he will be their God.' This is the language of marriage-covenant, wholehearted commitment of the 'one flesh' variety; God in you and you in God. Just as the Father, Son and Spirit are wrapped up in each other, one yet distinct, embracing each other in a wonderful dynamic of love, we too shall be caught up in what C.S. Lewis described as 'the great dance' of heaven. That is the future of a Christian believer.

Just look at what God will do in heaven: 'Wipe away every tear from our eyes.' The picture is a maternal one, like a mother tenderly lifting up her heartbroken child and dabbing away the tears streaming down its cheeks. Why tears? Apart from the fact that Christians like everyone else are bound up in this fallen world of death and suffering, which in heaven will be a thing of the past, they are also the objects of special suffering inflicted upon them because of their faith. We might think, for example, of a twenty-two-year-old girl called Perpetua who lived in North Africa in AD 203. With a baby at her breast she was martyred in the city of Carthage. Before her death she managed to write down her impressions. Her father had tried everything to make her renounce her faith. First he was rough with her. Then he appealed to his grey hairs, her mother, her baby who would not be able to survive without her. Nothing would cause her to flinch. Then she was killed. What was the first experience of Perpetua as she was ushered into the presence of God, her true Father? Tender comfort as she heard the words, 'It's all right Perpetua. You are safe now. You are home; home with your family, home with God.' Even in heaven, as on the cross, God still stoops down in holy humility to care for the needs of his children – that is the kind of God he is.

As God sees to the needs of his people, heaven is a place of *complete sufficiency*. 'He said to me: "It is done. I am the Alpha and the Omega, the Beginning and the End. To him who is thirsty I will give to drink without cost from the spring of the water of life. He who over-comes will inherit all this, and I will be his God and he will be my son"' (vv. 6–7). And then again in verses 22–6: 'I did not see a temple in the city, because the Lord God Almighty and the Lamb are its temple. The city does not need the sun or the moon to shine on it, for the glory of God gives it light, and the Lamb is its lamp. The nations will walk by its light, and the kings of the earth will bring their splendour into it. On no day will its gates ever be shut, for there will be no night there. The glory and honour of the nations will be brought into it.'

Even in heaven we will have needs. In paradise Adam had needs and God provided; in the new paradise also we will have needs, which God will provide for through his Son. 'He is the alpha and omega, the beginning and the end.' As his people we are hedged in on every side by his omnipotence. To those who are thirsty comes the invitation to drink from the spring of the water of life. Here on earth we now experience the rivers of life, which we are told in chapter 22 flow from the throne of God. In heaven we shall experience the source itself – the spring – for we shall be so close to God's throne that we shall be able to touch it. The majesty of God's love is something we shall not simply look upon in adoring wonder but something we shall be drinking, taking deep draughts of that love which will cause our souls to sparkle with unrestrained joy. Someone has put it like this: 'In a sense we already enjoy his love, even in the present life. But here it comes through the filter of providence, mixed with adversity and sorrow and distorted by the currents of demonic and human hatreds. There, it comes unmixed and undiluted, directly from its source in the very heart of God Himself.' Isn't that a marvellous thought? The most exhilarating church service we have ever attended, the richest, most moving time of prayer we have ever known will be but a memory of drab bleakness compared to the bathing in the divine love we shall know then.

Notice too, that there will be no need of a temple, that is the meeting place between God and man made possible by sacrifice. Why? Because the Lord God and the Lamb *are* the temple – the Father dwells with his children because of the sacrifice of Jesus the Lamb. We shall have immediate contact with God. Also there will be no need of sun or moon. Again we might ask, why? Because God himself will be all the light we need. The insecurities of the night – the time when thieves break in or wild animals attack – will be things of the past. In other words, no longer will God provide for us second-hand, as it were, but immediately and personally, for such is his love and commitment towards his church.

Which brings us to the next aspect of heaven: *absolute purity*. 'But the cowardly, the unbelieving, the vile, the murderers, the sexually immoral, those who practice magic arts, the idolaters and all liars – their place will be in the fiery lake of burning sulphur. This is the second death' (v. 8). Then in verse 27: 'Nothing impure will ever enter it, nor will anyone who does what is shameful or deceitful, but only those whose names are written in the Lamb's book of life.' What are the main concerns regarding our cities today? Are they not these: violence, theft, curb-crawling and prostitution, drunkenness, wanton damage to property, family breakdown? Why then should Laurie Lee try and turn these hellish features into virtues so as to make heaven out to be dull and dreary by way of contrast? Who would not want a city in which everyone spoke kindly to each other and delighted in each other's company? A place where women and children could walk the streets in complete safety? That is exactly what this city will be like: wholesome, clean, shining with absolute goodness and love. Far from this being the place for sad losers, an insipid, inane purgatory as the opponents of Christianity like George Bernard Shaw and Laurie Lee would have us believe, it is the very place men and women have dreamt of for centuries. Thomas More called it Utopia, but he made the mistake of thinking that it is an island we can build, rather than the paradise God restores and offers as a free gift to those who love his Son.

Finally, it is a place of *complete security*, which is what verses 9–21 convey with this vivid description of the dimensions and composition of the city.

To begin with, this city is a perfect cube which is reminiscent of the holy of holies of Solomon's temple (1 Kgs. 6:20). In other words, it is *all* temple. The *shekinah* glory which only occasionally appeared in the temple is absolutely everywhere, there is not one single moment when you are out of the presence of God, therefore being guaranteed his full and undivided attention and protection. We all have our fears and anxieties. Whatever they are they will have no place in heaven. As his people are covered with his presence, nothing evil will harm them, no temptation will lure them. We talk of sanctuary where a criminal can flee and not be molested by his pursuers. Here we are told that the holy city is *all* sanctuary, ensuring total protection for those who flee to Christ.

Secondly, this is a city that cannot be shaken because it is built upon the unshakeable and abiding word of God, his truth as proclaimed by the apostles: 'The wall of the city had twelve foundations, and on them where the names of the twelve apostles of the Lamb' (v. 14). For centuries the truth of the Gospel has been under attack. It happened in England during the Marian persecution of the Reformers; it happened in Nazi Germany under the might of the Third Reich; it happened in Russia under Communism and still it goes on. Yet the church has survived and has gone on from strength to strength as the truth of God's Word stands firm and does its work, leading people to Christ the Lamb. And so we can be sure that on that day not a single one of God's children will be missing who have embraced the message of the apostles. It is the truth of the Gospel which is the very foundation of heaven, so let us keep on believing it and proclaiming it.

Thirdly, this is Eden restored. All the components of the city are mentioned in Genesis 2 in the description of Eden – the gold, the precious jewels. Also they were used in the building of the tabernacle in the wilderness, the forerunner of the temple in Jerusalem. In other words, all that is precious, of value and beauty given for our delight will be there. What was lost by our rebellion will be restored in our redemption.

We end with an alternative description of heaven to that with which we began, one written by another great writer of English literature, C.S. Lewis. It comes at the end of 'The Last Battle', the final book in the Narnia series in which the Lion Aslan represents Christ, and the children – Lucy, Peter and the others – represent Christians. The children have been involved in a train accident in this world. They enter into the final days of Narnia when Aslan creates a new world:

> Aslan turned to them and said, 'You do not look as happy as you should be.' Lucy said, 'We're so afraid of being sent away, Aslan. And you have sent us back into our own world so often.' 'No fear of that,' said Aslan. 'Have you not guessed?' Their hearts leaped and a wild hope arose within them. 'There was a real railway accident,' said Aslan softly. 'Your father and mother and all of you are – as you used to call it in the Shadowlands – dead. The term is over: the holidays have begun. The dream is ended: this is the morning.' And as he spoke he no longer looked to them like a lion; but the things that began to happen after that were so great and beautiful that I cannot write them. And for us this is the end of all the stories, and we can most truly say that they all lived happily ever after. But for them it was only the beginning of the real story. All their life in this world and all their adventures in Narnia had only been the cover of the title page: now at last they were beginning Chapter 1 of the Great Story which no one on earth has read: which goes on for ever; in which every chapter is better than the one before.

Questions for Discussion

What is the Church?
Matthew 16:13–20

Getting Started . . .
1. What is the popular view of the church in today's society?
2. What do you think of when the 'church' is mentioned?

Getting it Right . . .
1. Why do you think Jesus asks his disciples about himself in verse 13?
2. What does Peter mean by his reply in verse 16?
3. How, according to Jesus, has Peter come to this understanding? (v. 17)
4. What does this say about spiritual knowledge and conversion?
5. In what sense is Peter the rock?
6. What is the job that Peter, and those who follow, are given? (v. 19)

Going Further . . .
1. Who makes up the church according to your study of this passage?
2. What does it mean for the church to be Jesus' church?

3. How will this change our often-held view of the church being 'our church'?
4. If the church is simply a gathering of people, how does this alter our view of 'church'?
5. What will it mean in terms of our attitude to one another, denominations, buildings, etc.?
6. What encouragement does Jesus offer in the fact that death cannot overtake the church?
7. If the church on earth is a representation of the heavenly one, what characteristics must we develop and show now?
8. In what sense is Peter's job our job?
9. Why should the Gospel be at the heart of every earthly gathering?
10. How has this study changed the way you think about church?

God and the Church
1 Peter 2:4–12

Getting Started . . .
1. Have you ever had to suffer for being a Christian, even in small ways? If so, how?
2. What kept you going as a Christian through these trials?

Going Further . . .
1. What does Peter say that God is doing with His people in verses 4–5?
2. What encouragement is there for the church that Jesus is the living stone in verse 4?
3. Peter calls the church a 'holy priesthood' in verse 5. In what ways might this be a challenge to you and your church?

4. What do verses 6–8 teach you about the different reactions to the Gospel message?
5. Peter says in verse 6 that the one who trusts in Jesus will never be put to shame. What confidence does this give you, if you trust in Jesus, as you face this life with all its uncertainties and troubles?
6. What warning is there for you in verses 7–8 if you disobey the message about Jesus?
7. What does Peter say in verses 9–10 about the Christian's status before God?
8. How do you think you can obey the command in verse 9 to declare God's praises?
9. How should your lifestyle affect the people around you, according to Peter in verses 11–12?
10. What changes do you think you would have to make to the way you act at home, at work or at college if you are to have an impact as Peter suggests?

The Marks of the Church
Acts 2:42–7

Getting Started . . .
1. What makes a 'successful' church in most people's eyes?
2. What do you think should be the marks of a healthy church?

Getting it Right . . .
1. In verses 37–41, what does Peter say is the proper response to the Gospel?
2. What role does the Holy Spirit play?
3. What were the characteristics of this church in verses 42–7?

Going Further . . .
1. Why do you think Luke puts teaching first? (v. 42)
2. How do you think this priority would show itself in a church today?
3. How would you define 'fellowship' from a passage like this?
4. How did this first church express their 'fellowship'? (vv. 44–5)
5. How does this compare to your own understanding of what 'fellowship' means?
6. What did this church do when they met together? (vv. 46–7)
7. What lessons can we learn about the way this church conducted themselves in their meetings together?
8. What do these lessons reveal about this church's attitude to God and to one another?
9. In what ways could you express your commitment to your local church?
10. What part did evangelism play in the life of this church?
11. How integral to the life of your church is evangelism?
12. What ways could you and your church seek to reach out to others in your local area?
13. If you were forced for some reason to move to another city, what criteria would you use to choose another church? Are they the right criteria?

The Calling of the Church
Ephesians 1:1–14

Getting Started . . .
1. Why is it that the non-Christian world so often looks on the church with such disdain?

2. Why do Christians often adopt this view of church?

Getting it Right . . .
1. According to Paul what does the Christian lack? (v. 3)
2. What blessings does Paul mention here that are ours in Christ?
3. What phrases keep cropping up in the passage?
4. What do they tell us about these blessings?

Going Further . . .
1. What does Paul say about the church's election? (vv. 4–5, 11)
2. What confidence does this give you as a believer to press on in the world?
3. What does Paul say about the church's identification? (v. 4)
4. How will this identification 'in Christ' show itself in your daily life?
5. How does Paul say that God has redeemed his church? (v. 7)
6. What does this reveal about God's commitment to his people?
7. Why does Paul say that the church is 'for the praise of God's glory' in verse 12?
8. How can you and your church respond to this challenge?

Building Up the Church
Ephesians 4:1–16

Getting Started . . .
1. If you were dreaming of the ideal church, what would it be like?

2. Why do you think many churches have so many problems?

Going Further . . .

The Church's Unity

1. What does it mean to live a life worthy of the calling we have received? (v. 1)
2. How will this show itself in practice?
3. Which qualities in verse 2 do you find hardest to live out?
4. How can we become better at living them out?
5. Why should we bother to make every effort to keep the unity of the Spirit? (v. 3)

The Church's Diversity

1. What does Paul say Jesus has given the church? (vv. 7–11)
2. How are we to be prepared for service? (v. 12)
3. How can you support your pastor in his God-given task?
4. How do you think you can be involved in these works of service in your local church?

The Church's Maturity

1. What is the ultimate goal of the church? (v. 13)
2. How will this be achieved?
3. What will it mean in practice for you to become mature in the faith?
4. Paul uses the illustration of the body in verses 15–16. What does this teach you about your local church? How will you play your part?

The Model Church
1 Thessalonians 1

Getting Started . . .
1. Who have been the people in your life that have modelled to you the Christian faith?
2. What Christian characteristics did they model to you?

Going Further . . .
1. What understanding of 'church' does Paul have in verse 1?
2. How does this compare with your view of 'church'?
3. What qualities do the Thessalonians have according to Paul in verse 3?
4. Do you think these are qualities of the 'normal Christian life'? If so, why?
5. In what practical ways could you develop these qualities in your personal life and in your life together as church?
6. Paul is convinced that this church in Thessalonica is a genuine church. What evidence for this does he mention in verses 5–8?
7. If Paul were to take a look at your church life, would he find similar evidence? If not, what changes do you think need to be made?
8. What links does Paul make between the 'word' of the Gospel and the Holy Spirit in verses 5–6?
9. What does this tell us about evangelism?
10. Verses 9–10 are often thought to be a summary of the Thessalonians' experience. What do these verses show us about the start and the content of the Christian life?
11. Ask yourself these three questions honestly: Have I turned from idols? Am I serving the living God? Am I waiting for Jesus' return?

The Care of the Church
Acts 20:17–38

Getting Started . . .
1. What expectations do you have of your church leaders?
2. Do you think they are realistic?

Going Further . . .

The Model of Caring

1. What qualities does Paul show as a model pastor?
2. How did these qualities work in practice in Paul's ministry with the Ephesians? (vv. 18–19 and 33–5)
3. In what ways could you show these qualities in your Christian life?

The Method of Caring

1. How might you sum up Paul's methods in caring for his church? (v. 20)
2. How did these methods work in practice? (vv. 20–1, 27, 32)
3. What dangers does Paul outline for the Ephesian ministers? (vv. 29ff.)
4. Do you agree that there is a possibility that an evangelical minister could become a 'wolf'? If so, why?
5. How should a minister stop himself going down this track?
6. How can you help in this process?
7. Paul is writing chiefly for ministers, but how might some of these methods be applied in our homes and families?

The Motivation for Caring

1. What is Paul's motivation for ministry? (vv. 24, 28a)
2. How might this be a motivation for us in any church work we are involved in?
3. If you were on an interviewing panel for choosing the next minister, how would this passage affect your decision?

Worship in the Church
Hebrews 12:18 – 13:21

Getting Started . . .
1. How would you define 'worship'?
2. What evidence from the Bible could you present to defend your definition?

Going Further . . .
1. To what degree does the understanding of worship as 'engaging with God' challenge your view of worship?
2. Looking at Hebrews 9:1–7, how did the Old Testament people of God 'engage with God'?
3. What is the trouble with this way of doing things?
4. How do some Christians reflect this 'BC' way of engaging with God? What is wrong with these ways?
5. How has the coming of Jesus changed the way we 'engage with God'? To help answer this, look up Hebrews 1:1–4 and 10:19–22.
6. What will this mean for special priests or buildings or rituals and the like?
7. What does Hebrews 12:22–6 tell us about our privilege as New Testament Christians?

8. Read through Hebrews 13. What different things does the writer teach you about 'worshipping' God?
9. Which of these do you think you need to work on in particular?
10. How has this study changed the way you think about 'worship'? Are you a BC or an AD Christian?

Prayer in the Church
Acts 4:23–31

Getting Started ...
1. Why do you think prayer has such a low profile in many churches in our country? How might this be changed?
2. What excuses do we give for not praying in our personal lives and in our church life? Are they valid?

Going Further ...

God-Centred Priorities

1. What was the initial reaction of the apostles and the church when they heard about the events of chapter 4, verse 1–22? (and 23–4)
2. What does this reveal about this first church's priorities?
3. What is your initial reaction when faced with a serious problem?
4. What stops you from praying in these sorts of situations?

God-Centred Understanding

1. What did this church understand by God's sovereignty? (v. 24)
2. What do you understand by God's sovereignty?
3. How had God shown his sovereignty in recent history? (vv. 25–8)
4. Why was it important for this church to know that God was sovereign?
5. How will knowing this about God affect your own prayer life?
6. What difference do you think it would make if you ignored this about God?

God-Centred Request

1. What was the church's request in verses 29–30?
2. What would you have prayed in this situation?
3. What do these requests say about this church's aims and desires?
4. How do your prayers compare to this church's?
5. If you wanted your church congregation to become more like this early church in its prayer life what changes would you have to make?
6. What changes would you personally have to make?

The Influence of the Church
Matthew 5:13–16

Getting Started ...
1. How much influence do you think Christians can have in the world?

2. Why do you think Christians are often reluctant to be salt and light in the world?

Going Further . . .
1. What does Jesus imply about the world when he says that Christians are to be salt and light? Do you think this is a fair assessment?
2. What examples can you think of which show that this world is rotting and dark? Think of examples both on a global scale, and also on a more local scale.
3. Why is it important for Christians to have a proper understanding of the nature of the world today?
4. What do you think Jesus means when he says 'you are the salt of the earth' in verse 13?
5. In what practical ways could you apply Jesus' teaching in your own life?
6. How might you be in danger of 'losing your saltiness'?
7. What steps could you take to prevent this from happening?
8. How can you be the light of the world, as Jesus says in verse 14?
9. Are you ever tempted to hide your light? If so why?
10. What incentive is there for us in verse 16 to be the light of the world?
11. How much influence do you now think Christians can have in the world?

The Future of the Church
Revelation 21

Getting Started . . .
1. What do you think of when you think of heaven?

2. How big a part does heaven play in your thinking as a Christian?

Going Further . . .

1. John tells us in verse 5 that God says he is making everything 'new'. Why is the fact that everything is new so thrilling for us as Christians?
2. What do we discover that heaven is all about in this passage?
3. How does John describe heaven in verse 2?
4. What do each of these descriptions tell us about heaven?
5. How does God's purpose for his people come to fulfilment in verse 3?
6. How might the truths of verses 3–7 spur you on to live the Christian life now?
7. What does the central section in verses 9–21 add to John's vision of heaven?
8. How might the picture of heaven in Revelation 21 affect the way you view church now?
9. How has this passage changed your view of heaven?
10. Why is this hope of heaven as revealed in Revelation 21 so important to Christians?
11. What steps can you take to make this hope of heaven a greater part of your Christian life?

Further Reading

Colson, Charles (with Ellen Santilli Vaughn), *The Body: Being Light in Darkness* (Milton Keynes: Word, 1992)

Griffiths, Michael, *Cinderella With Amnesia* (London: IVP, 1975)

Jackman, David, *Understanding the Church* (Fearn: Mentor, 1996)

MacArthur, Jr, John, *The Master's Plan for the Church* (Chicago: Moody, 1991)

Peterson, David, *Engaging with God* (Leicester: Apollos, 1992)

Roberts, Vaughan, *True Worship* (Carlisle: Paternoster, 2002)